Complete
Copyright

FOR K–12 LIBRARIANS AND EDUCATORS

Complete Copyright

FOR K–12 LIBRARIANS AND EDUCATORS

Carrie Russell

A PROJECT OF THE OFFICE FOR INFORMATION TECHNOLOGY POLICY

American Library Association | Chicago 2012

Published 2012 by the American Library Association

Illustrations © 2012 by Jessica Abel

This publication is not meant as legal advice. It was prepared to inform librarians and the public about copyright. The views expressed are those of the authors, not of their employers or affiliated organizations. While extensive effort has gone into ensuring the reliability of the information in this book, the publisher makes no warranty, express or implied, with respect to the material contained herein.

ISBNs: 978-0-8389-1083-2 (paper); 978-0-8389-9574-7 (PDF).

Library of Congress Cataloging-in-Publication Data
Russell, Carrie.
   Complete copyright for K-12 librarians and educators / Carrie Russell.
      p. cm.
   Includes bibliographical references and index.
   ISBN 978-0-8389-1083-2 (alk. paper)
   1. Copyright—United States. 2. Fair use (Copyright)—United States. 3. School libraries—Law and legislation—United States. 4. Librarians—Legal status, laws, etc.—United States. I. Title.
   KF2995.R87 2012
   346.7304'820240278—dc23   2012016674

Cover illustration by Jessica Abel. Book design in Denim, Triplex Sans, and Matrix II by Kirstin Krutsch.

♾ This paper meets the requirements of ANSI/NISO Z39.48-1992 (Permanence of Paper).

Printed in the United States of America
16 15 14 13 12   5 4 3 2 1

CONTENTS

PREFACE

Digital technology and networks have changed our society—how we communicate with one another, how we purchase goods, how we work together to create reference resources, how we more willingly give up anonymity and allow invasions of privacy, how we read, how we teach. Particularly in places of learning, technology is all-pervasive, and because everyone is always making copies, copyright is center stage. History shows us that during times of technological change, copyright goes through a period of adjustment as it tries to keep pace with the technology. Copyright never catches up to technology. Consistency can be found only in our dedication to professional values.

Although some predicted that the new digital environment would signal the end of libraries, it turned out to be just the opposite, because in countless ways the introduction of digital technology has been the beginning of libraries. Others argue that copyright is an outdated law that does not work in the digital environment, but it is still with us and is still important. It's just a little more complicated.

Prior to this technological change, librarians were one of the select groups even interested in copyright law. We had to be interested to protect access to information and other public policies that are central to librarianship. Today, educators should be interested in copyright to protect learning, because copyright law when misapplied or misinterpreted affects the way that you teach and even *what* you teach. This book seeks to address the concerns of librarians, teachers, and teaching librarians who work in the K–12 environment.

To tackle this task, I will use library and teaching scenarios to illustrate copyright situations. This was a key component of *Complete Copyright: An Everyday Guide for Librarians*, and people said they liked it. Many of these scenarios involve actual questions that librarians have asked me over the last several years. My "Carrie on Copyright" column in *School Library Journal* has produced a lot of fodder, and lurking on discussion lists to collect copyright stories has also been helpful in gaining an understanding of what school librarians and teachers are doing in the classroom or what they want to do. For good measure, I conducted an informal survey of librarians to gain a sense of their concerns and attitudes about copyright. More than 280 librarians responded to the survey. (The complete survey and results are in appendix A.) This data collection has supported my contention that school librarians tend to have a fear of copyright litigation, leading them to make overly conservative decisions. I also discovered that many of the copyright reference tools used by the K–12 community are either incomplete or not correct. Digging into the past, some of the copyright materials you have received over the years from vendors, publishers, and yes, ALA, have sidestepped any mention of public policy and how librarians and educators should think about copyright. It is actually a law that seeks to help us teach and learn.

My hope is that this book will make copyright understandable and that, with new-found confidence, you will be able to make copyright decisions that are both lawful and in the best interests of your learning community. But because you are professionals with a commitment to the information rights of the public, you must be able to do more than just answer the copyright questions that come to you.

Unlike many other copyright books, this book will challenge old assumptions that you may hold dear. This book will encourage you to embrace the purpose of the copyright law and to be committed to preserving that purpose. As you develop copyright policies and educational materials, this book is going to push you to make more long-term strategic decisions that will see you through changes in the law, rather than taking the easy way out. This book will encourage you to stop running away from copyright out of some tenuous fear of litigation and instead be more involved in shaping copyright law to better serve your learning community. Your attention to copyright should be as profound as your interest in censorship—both are central to the freedom of speech.

ACKNOWLEDGMENTS

Writing this book would not have been achievable without the support and expertise of many other individuals. In particular, I would like to thank my colleagues Alan Inouye and Larra Clark for reading earlier versions of the book and providing overall editorial feedback as well as the occasional reality check. I am grateful to school librarians Janet Schultz and Stacy Vogel for their feedback on my early attempts to explain copyright in an interesting and understandable way that would resonate with K–12 librarians and educators. Jonathan Band conducted a legal review of the book and was always available to address any specific legal questions I had along the way. I am immensely fortunate to know and work with such a brilliant lawyer. I was lucky to work again with the talented illustrator Jessica Abel, whose creativity adds enormously to this book on the somewhat dry topic of copyright. Finally, I would like to thank my work colleagues for their fellowship and interest. There were many times when I was asked, "How's the book coming along?"—which became increasingly annoying as time passed, especially when I was not making much progress. This book is dedicated to them just to get them off of my back.

CAST OF CHARACTERS

Gary LeDuc

Gary LeDuc is a representative of the Copyright Compliance and Anti-Piracy Division of Homeland Security. He presents a program on copyright for the teachers, librarians, and administrators for the school district. Unfortunately, Gary is a copyright maximalist and has a limited view of fair use. He tends to talk too loudly. On the plus side, Gary does like animals.

Lindsey Eagen Hancock

Lindsey Eagen Hancock is a newly graduated "information science specialist." She has a tendency to see the world from her perspective only—either you're wrong or Lindsey's right. Lindsey loves rules and loves to enforce rules even more. With time, Lindsey will become a first-rate librarian. She just needs to stop talking about herself all the time. On weekends, Lindsey does volunteer work. She is a great baker of fruit pies.

Cliff Chmielewski

Cliff Chmielewski is one of the school district's IT employees. He is smart and committed to helping teachers, librarians, and students understand and use technology. A longtime fan of Marshall McLuhan, Cliff believes that technology can solve just about any problem. He has a "presence" in Second Life, but his Second Life tends to be more active than his real life. Cliff has many gamer friends, and maybe too many RSS feeds. His favorite show is *Battlestar Galactica*. He owns a book autographed by Larry Lessig.

Patrick Monahan

Patrick Monahan is a creative guy with a wicked sense of humor. He is a reader of graphic novels and wants to be an illustrator. He DJs at dance parties and loves music and mash-ups. Patrick has already written three different endings to Cory Doctorow's *For the Win*. Socially mature for his age and a leader by nature, Patrick manages to be cool without ever acting superior.

Kim Pickel

As the school principal, Kim Pickel provides leadership by focusing on the needs of the students. She is a straight talker and makes decisions based on practicality. Kim has only a few close friends who have managed to penetrate her somewhat detached facade. Most people don't know that Kim is a regular at the neighborhood karaoke bar, belting out show tunes like nobody's business.

Lola Lola

Lola Lola, head librarian at Wessex University, is a real library leader. She mentors her staff, works collegially with faculty, and is inspired by change and new ideas. When not fighting for fair use, Lola is busy writing her sixth mystery novel, *Murder in the Closed Stacks*.

Lena Valez

Thanks to budget cuts, Lena Valez is the school librarian at both Miles Elementary and Glen Valley High School. It's only in the last year that Lena has begun to contemplate retirement. Perhaps being a busy and productive librarian and president of the state library association is becoming just too much of a grind. She still enjoys her job, but she needs to learn how to say no sometimes. A fourteen-day Mediterranean cruise sounds pretty good right now.

Veronda Taylor

Veronda Taylor transferred to Glen Valley High School after a five-year stint as a fifth-grade teacher at Miles. She's well liked and hip, and her colleagues appreciate her energy, fresh ideas, and willingness to lend a helping hand. Her six-month sabbatical as a field consultant for the "Building Digital Inclusive Communities" initiative at the Institute of Museums and Library Services begins this spring.

Glen Valley
High School
Home of the Grizzlies!

Glen Valley High School is the Miles Union School District's largest high school, serving 1,423 students in grades 8–12. As the fall semester gets under way, teachers are refining their curricula in partnership with the school librarians, students have high expectations that the Glen Valley Grizzly football team will win the division title, a December talent show is in the planning stages, and the renovated library media center will have a grand-opening celebration.

Our story begins at a districtwide professional development day, where a copyright workshop is being conducted by a representative of the Copyright Permissions Corporation.

CHAPTER 1
Staff Attend a Copyright Workshop

This year, the Copyright Permissions Corporation has sent Gary LeDuc, a copyright expert, to meet with teachers and librarians over the next few days to provide copyright advice. This is a rare opportunity for the school district to get some accurate information about copyright law.

COPYRIGHT MYTHS AND MISCONCEPTIONS

Why do librarians and teachers—the very professionals who specialize in information literacy, equitable access to information, and the advancement of learning—have so many misconceptions about copyright? I have several theories that will be explored throughout this book, but one thing is certain—school librarians have many misconceptions about copyright, and many who have a guarded approach to copyright harbor an unfounded fear of copyright litigation. Rather safe than sorry is a frequent assertion. Philosophical copyright concepts—freedom of expression, the advancement of learning, the free flow of information—are not the focus of contemplation or discussion. Instead, most K–12 librarians expect and desire definitive answers to copyright questions even when no definitive answers exist. A copyright cheat sheet with yes and no answers is preferred—even if the answers are wrong.

School librarians and teachers are not to blame. Copyright is a subject barely mentioned in library school or education programs. Most of the copyright education materials targeted to the K–12 environment are wrong or woefully incomplete.[1] And copyright law is complicated. Part of the hesitancy on the part of librarians to assert users' rights to information comes from the school environment itself. Staff are dedicated but spread thin, already overburdened with work, assignments, lesson plans, grading, and staff meetings. People lack the time to deal with copyright. Moreover, school librarians are usually on their own as the sole librarian for the school—without other professional librarians around on a day-to-day basis to talk to about copyright. Yet there is the expectation that librarians in particular should have a deeper understanding of copyright and that librarians and teachers should model lawful uses of protected works as an example to the students they teach.

How can we learn about copyright and be more confident when providing copyright advice to teachers and students? Hopefully, this book will provide some answers. The annual copyright training session is not going to do the trick. Understanding copyright is a process, not a onetime event. Applying copyright has much to do with the "copyright attitude" of your institution. Is your institution focused on limiting risk of liability? Sometimes history, state law, school board decisions, and administrator whims influence the crafting of library copyright policy and how things are done. Entering into a continuing dialogue about copyright with teachers, staff, and administrators in your school is necessary to develop sound copyright policy. The copyright handout with "yes, you can" and usually more "no, you can't" guidelines also will not work. The quick-and-dirty approach to copyright is shortsighted, with long-term, negative implications. It can be a disservice not only to students, by conflicting with the school's educational mission, but also to librarians, who risk abandoning their professional values.

To manage copyright effectively in your school, begin by understanding the purpose of the copyright law. Learn basic concepts—exclusive rights, public domain, requirements for protection—and apply all available exceptions under the law to the advantage of your school community. Make informed decisions, but accept ambiguity. Consider yoga classes, breathe deeply, and clear your mind of copyright misinformation.

TOP FIVE COPYRIGHT MISCONCEPTIONS

Misconception 1: Copyright law exists to ensure that authors and other creators are compensated monetarily for the works they create.

In a web-based survey I conducted of school librarians, 82.7 percent of those that responded said they believed author compensation was the purpose of the copyright law.[2] But the U.S. Constitution says that copyright law is created "to promote the Progress of Science and useful Arts."[3] Thus the intent of the copyright law is, first and foremost, to encourage the creation and dissemination of original, creative works that benefit the public. Copyright policy seeks to advance the public's welfare by making works available that promote learning, inspire the creation of new works, produce well-informed citizens, and foster the pursuit of happiness.[4] Of particular importance to the founders of the country was the goal of a well-informed citizenry. To effectively participate in a democratic system, all citizens must have the necessary access to knowledge, information, and creative works.

Creative and original works, of course, do not rise from the ether. Creative and talented people use their labor to create these works and are provided an incentive to disseminate them to the public. To encourage the creation of new works, Congress allows authors, creators, and other rights holders the legal right to a monopoly, with some limitations. This monopoly, defined by Congress, is realized by awarding to the author a set of economic rights, exclusive to the author or other rights holder. In the simplest of terms, rights holders have sole authority to market their works. This is the bargain struck between the public—who require and enjoy access to information—and the author or rights holder—who seeks compensation for creating and disseminating creative expressions.

U.S. copyright is unlike the copyright laws of civil law countries (in Europe and elsewhere) because its central focus is a *utilitarian* one. Rather than focusing on the "natural" right of authors to control works that are a result of their intellectual creativity and achievement, we focus on economic incentives to serve a specific public purpose. It is therefore incorrect to say that an author's work innately "belongs" to her, at least in a U.S. context. Instead, copyright is granted to an author by Congress as an incentive to create and disseminate.[5]

The notion that copyright law serves the public interest may sound quaint today, when much of the public discussion and certainly much of political debate is about the monetary value of copyright. Copyright does have an important economic value in the global information economy. But the fundamental purpose of U.S. copyright law continues to be the public's welfare. The values that underlie the copyright law are completely consistent with the professional values of teachers and librarians. Asserting those values for the benefit of your library and school communities as you interpret and apply the copyright law is appropriate because it furthers the law's objectives.

Misconception 2: Rights holders sue libraries, teachers, and schools all the time.

Rest easy. Actual court cases involving libraries and schools are extremely rare.[6] We tend to believe that libraries or schools are frequently in trouble with the law because we hear about schools that have been threatened with a lawsuit. Most of the time, the threat of a lawsuit is enough to make a school terminate a behavior that is an alleged infringement. A cease and desist letter and payment of a license fee is not copyright infringement. Infringement is only determined by a court hearing a real infringement claim.

Still, you may be worried about breaking the law and being held responsible for your actions or the actions of teachers or students. There are several reasons why these fears are not warranted.

First—because copyright law ultimately seeks to benefit the public, uses of protected works for teaching, research and scholarship, and learning are favored under the law. These socially beneficial uses are often reflected in the law as exceptions—limitations to the rights of the copyright holder that allow the public (or certain entities) the right to use a work in ways that would otherwise be infringing. These limitations are necessary because they aid in containing the copyright monopoly. If the monopoly created by the Congress were all-encompassing, the purpose of the law—to advance learning and culture for the public's welfare—could not be achieved.

Socially beneficial uses tend to occur more frequently in libraries, schools, and institutions of higher education because these are places where learners gather and knowledge is shared. In particular, these institutions (occasionally along with archives, museums, historical societies, and other cultural institutions) hold special status under the law in that more limitations are created by Congress to address their unique need to serve the public, provide equitable access to information, and preserve the cultural record.

Second—in the unlikely event that a school or library is taken to court for alleged infringement, the rights holder cannot expect to win a large monetary award. Congress has set up special limits on penalties that are set at trial if a school or library is found to have infringed copyright.

> The court shall remit statutory damages in any case where an infringer believed and had reasonable grounds for believing that his or her use of the copyrighted work was a fair use under section 107, if the infringer was: (i) an employee or agent of a nonprofit educational institution, library, or archives acting within the scope of his or her employment who, or such institution, library, or archives itself, which infringed by reproducing the work in copies or phonorecords.[7]

These two major allowances—exceptions to exclusive rights and limits on remedies—granted by Congress to nonprofit educational institutions and libraries point to their privileged status under copyright law.

Finally—public educational institutions and libraries are protected by the Eleventh Amendment to the U.S. Constitution.[8] The Eleventh Amendment says that state entities cannot be sued in a federal court without their consent. Again, this places a limit on the remedies that rights holders could expect to collect if they sue schools or libraries.

Misconception 3: Original, creative expressions protected by copyright law are the property of their creators or rights holders.

People are often confused or are led to believe that copyright law is the same as a property law. This confusion is compounded by the use of terms like "intellectual property," which is a misnomer.[9] Instead, copyright law resembles government regulation in that Congress creates the law to intervene in the free market by granting rights holders a monopoly—via exclusive rights of copyright—to achieve a public purpose. If one assumes that copyright is a property law, this can lead to the assumption that creative works are "owned" by rights holders and therefore any unauthorized use of "their property" is forbidden.[10] This in turn leads to the use of words like "stealing" and "piracy" when the correct term for violating the copyright law is "infringement." Why is this distinction so important? Because we immediately understand that stealing is immoral and wrong, while some kinds of uses of works without the authority of the rights holder are lawful and indeed necessary to promote the progress of science and useful arts.

Creative works also are unique in their nature in that they cannot be used up, and it is difficult to exclude others from them. Economists say that these traits—nonrivalry and non-exclusivity—are characteristics of "public goods." When I listen to music, I do not consume music in the same way that I consume an apple. The music is still available to anyone else to listen to, while the apple has been eaten up. Another unique trait of creative works is that they gain value the more they are used. You cannot wear them out like a pair of shoes. The more information is shared and used, the more knowledgeable people become and the more new knowledge is created. These distinctions are not just mere curiosities. They help us better understand the benefit of creative works to the public.[11]

Misconception 4: There are a set of legal rules that give definitive answers to copyright questions.

Not true, and this is what many librarians and teachers find vexing. Often the answer to a specific copyright query requires that one analyze the situation at hand to make a determination—in other words, determine if the use is fair. (Fair use will be discussed further throughout this book.) You could make up a set of rules that must be followed and that in essence become definitive answers by continuing practice—and there are many examples out there—but these would be arbitrary rules without the force and effect of law.[12] It is actually in our best interests to have ambiguity in the law. To set copyright rules in stone would be to "freeze" the law.[13] The law must be malleable to serve us now and in the future, a future that we can only speculate on. Fair use will serve us well because it is more open to new technologies.

Some of the exceptions to copyright law—like section 108 (library reproductions) or section 110 (public performances for educational and other purposes) are more definite than fair use. If your use falls within these exceptions, it is always permitted. However, these exceptions are relatively rigid and don't necessarily address all situations that may

From: Gary LeDuc <leduc@crpc.org>
Sent: Fri 3:47 PM CST
Subject: **Today's presentation on copyright**
To: Lindsey Eagen Hancock <lindsey@glenvalley.miles.k-12.wi.us>

Dear Lindsey:

I am so glad to hear that you enjoyed the copyright presentation! I share your concerns about potential infringing activities taking place here at Glen Valley. You are correct—copyright compliance is everyone's responsibility. I look forward to providing any assistance that I can while I visit the school over the next two days.

Regards,

GL

....
Gary LeDuc, Director of Outreach Education
Copyright Permissions Corporation
US Department of Homeland Security
Washington, DC

confront a teacher or librarian. Section 108 addresses preservation, replacement, interlibrary loan, copies of works for library users—but it doesn't address when you can reproduce an image on the Internet for your library home page. It doesn't address whether you can make a reproduction for a student who is learning English as a second language. It doesn't address whether you can make a copy of a page from a book to replace a missing page in your damaged copy. You get the idea.

It is not easy for some to deal with the ambiguity of fair use and the complex elements of specific copyright exceptions. Many of us like rules—can I do this or not?—but to be an effective librarian or teacher dealing with copyright requires that you bite the bullet, learn the four factors of fair use and apply them, and accept (and maybe appreciate) gaps in the law. It is a strength of our copyright law that it has both definite exceptions as well as flexible exceptions.

Misconception 5: Fair use is too difficult to understand and apply.

Not so. Once you learn the four factors of fair use, making a fair use determination comes more naturally, although it is never definitive.[14] A court of law makes the final call on whether some action is fair or not, but because we aren't in litigation over every fair use, we must learn to make our own decisions, even when we cannot be absolutely certain that we are 100 percent correct. You do not have to have a law degree to conclude that a use is fair. Nor should you consult a lawyer or higher authority every time you need to determine fair use. It is your professional responsibility to understand fair use because your role is to facilitate access to and use of information. Your underlying commitment to the public is to ensure that their rights are fully explored. Fair use is the best way to balance user rights with the interests of rights holders.

Librarians and teachers are not to blame in having these misconceptions. Information distributed to librarians over the years has been wrong or incomplete, and often conflicting. The software industry prepared several copyright education guides for librarians written with a focus, naturally, on software piracy. User rights were not a highlight of these documents, which instead highlighted the position that librarians should take the role of copyright police for the school and report software license infractions.[15]

In an educational video published by one coalition, the link between copyright infringement and stealing property is made at the outset.[16] Copyright infringement at school is just like the driver's education teacher stealing a school car, the narrator asserts. Librarians are urged to work with their vendors on copyright compliance to keep prices low. Fair use is mentioned but described incorrectly—we are told that all four factors must be fair in order for the use to be fair. Librarians are urged to "exercise caution"—advised that it's probably best to ask permission all of the time. The threat of litigation is introduced, with the narrator warning that if the school were sued, the individuals involved in the alleged infringement would be sued as well. One would assume after watching this video that users had very few rights under the law.

Even the American Library Association, in its educational materials produced in the 1980s and 1990s, misdirected librarians to focus on guidelines rather than on a full understanding of what the copyright law is.[17] Throughout the drafting of the Copyright Act of 1976, librarians asked Congress for more clarity on what they and their library users could lawfully reproduce. The gorilla in the room at the time was the photocopy machine. Most libraries had photocopy machines, and of course, the public was using them. Librarians wanted clear instructions to solve their immediate problem rather than focusing on longer-term solutions based on the interests of their user community. Of course, hindsight is 20/20, but by emphasizing compliance, many librarians demonstrated a lack of foresight and a willingness to give up decision making to the publishers. ALA and other library associations fought hard for the library exceptions included in the Copyright Act, but librarians on the front line still wanted clarity. Publishers and authors, who were concerned that libraries would start copying everything, were happy to develop "fair use guidelines" as models for libraries, but unfortunately, these guidelines were never used as Congress intended. The widespread use of fair use guidelines led in part to misconceptions about fair use. Very few librarians knew the four factors of fair use.

Another reason these misconceptions exist is because most schools still do not focus on copyright education for their librarians and teachers.[18] And it can be difficult to find a copyright instructor who presents a balanced approach to the subject. Too often, when librarians do attend a copyright workshop, they note that no two copyright instructors seem to say the same thing, making it difficult to know whom to believe and what one should do. And there's a myriad of information on copyright on the Web, often also contradictory, leading to more confusion.

Finally, librarians and teachers—in part to deal with the confusion—have surrendered to reliance on checklists—hard-and-fast rules that tell you what to do, not how to think. Checklists, by their very nature, have an audit quality—when you use a checklist you look for things that are on the list or must be checked for compliance. If something is not checked off, the assumption is that the action is unlawful or, at least, against the rules of the school. Checklists, over time, become "the copyright law" to many people and greatly limit one's ability to teach.

KEY LEARNINGS

In *The Cost of Copyright Confusion for Media Literacy*, an ethnographic study of educators that teach information and media literacy skills, the authors report that "too many teachers fear they will misinterpret fair use or are simply unaware of its expansive nature."[19] Teachers report that at least some of their copyright fears are based on what they have been told by their librarians. Librarians are described as "sticklers" or "copyright police," taking it upon themselves to enforce copyright rules. This perception, whether true or not, should give us pause to rethink how we are managing copyright in our schools. If we are the copyright experts at our schools, we had better know what we are doing.[20] Our copyright misconceptions have led us to believe that copyright law is first and foremost about infringement. This is wrong. The copyright law serves our community by promoting the advancement of learning. Of course, we have a role in ensuring that copyright law is followed, but that responsibility should not lead to an overcompliance that limits the information rights of the people we serve. Instead, we should help our teachers and students use information to the broadest extent possible under the law.

NOTES

1. Some of the better copyright education materials can be found on college and university library and other websites. These resources are applicable for the K–12 school environment with minor revisions.
2. "SLMS and Copyright" was a survey sent to subscribers of the LM_NET discussion list in May 2008. Results of the survey, which garnered 284 responses, can be found in appendix A.
3. "The Congress shall have Power . . . To promote the Progress of Science and useful Arts, by securing for limited Times to Authors and Inventors the exclusive Right to their respective Writings and Discoveries." U.S. Const. art. I, § 8.
4. See L. Ray Patterson and Stanley W. Lindberg, *The Nature of Copyright: A Law of Users' Rights* (Athens: University of Georgia Press, 1991); Lydia Pallas Loren, "The Purpose of Copyright," *Open Spaces Quarterly* 2, no. 1 (February 1999), www.open-spaces.com/issue-v2n1.php.
5. "The limited scope of the copyright holder's statutory monopoly, like the limited copyright duration required by the Constitution, reflects a balance of competing claims upon the public interest: Creative work is to be created and rewarded, but private motivation must ultimately serve the cause of promoting broad public availability of literature, music and the other arts." *Twentieth Century Music Corp. v. Aiken*, 422 U.S. 151, 156 (1975).
6. To the best of my knowledge, there is only one—*Encyclopaedia Britannica v. Crooks*, 542 F. Supp. 1156 (W.D.N.Y. 1982).
7. Copyright Act of 1976, 17 U.S.C. § 504(c)(2).

8. "The Judicial power of the United States shall not be construed to extend to any suit in law or equity, commenced or prosecuted against one of the United States by Citizens of another State, or by Citizens or Subjects of any Foreign State." U.S. Const. amend. XI.

9. Mark Lemley believes the term "intellectual property" became a common descriptor beginning with the World Intellectual Property Organization in the 1980s. Mark A. Lemley, "Property, Intellectual Property, and Free Riding," *Texas Law Review* 83, no. 4 (2005): 1033n4. I think intellectual property is a misnomer because exclusive rights of copyright are not the same as property rights. I do not encourage the use of the term.

10. *Dowling v. United States*, 473 U.S. 207, 216, 217 (1985). "The copyright owner, however, holds no ordinary chattel. A copyright, like other intellectual property, comprises a series of carefully defined and carefully delimited interests to which the law affords correspondingly exact protections. . . . It follows that interference with copyright does not easily equate with theft, conversion, or fraud."

11. "If nature has made any one thing less susceptible than all others of exclusive property, it is the action of the thinking power called an idea, which an individual may exclusively possess as long as he keeps it to himself; but the moment it is divulged, it forces itself into the possession of every one, and the receiver cannot dispossess himself of it. . . . He who receives an idea from me, receives instructions himself without lessening mine; as he who lights his taper at mine, receives light without darkening me. That ideas should freely spread from one to another over the globe, for the moral and mutual instruction of man, and improvement of his condition, seems to have been peculiarly and benevolently designed by nature." Thomas Jefferson, *The Writings of Thomas Jefferson*, vol. 6, ed. H. A. Washington (Washington, DC, 1854), 180.

12. Such as the "Agreement on Guidelines for Classroom Copying in Not-for-Profit Educational Institutions with Respect to Books and Periodicals" (see appendix B) or the "Fair Use Guidelines for Educational Multimedia" (see appendix G).

13. "[Section 107] endorses the purpose and general scope of the judicial doctrine of fair use, but there is no disposition to freeze the doctrine in the statute, especially during a period of rapid technological change. Beyond a very broad statutory explanation of what fair use is and some of the criteria applicable to it, the courts must be free to adapt the doctrine to particular situations on a case-by-case basis. Section 107 is intended to restate the present judicial doctrine of fair use, not to change, narrow, or enlarge it in any way." H.R. Rep. No. 94-1476, at 66 (1976).

14. Fair use will be explored in chapter 3.

15. *The K–12 Guide to Legal Software Use* (Washington, DC: Software Publishing Association, 1994), *Don't Copy That Floppy* (VHS) (Washington, DC: Software Publishing Association, 1992), and *It Could Be So Easy* (VHS) (Washington, DC: Software Publishing Association, 1995). See also "You Wouldn't Steal a Car," a 2004 advertisement by the Motion Picture Association of America.

16. The coalition was called F.A.C.T. (Folks Against Copyright Transgressions). *Copyright Law: What Every School, College and Public Library Should Know* (VHS) (Northbrook, IL: AIME, 1987).

17. American Library Association, "ALA Model Policy Concerning College and University Photocopying for Classroom, Research, and Library Reserve Use," *College and Research Library News* 43 (1982): 127–31.

18. Of the librarians I surveyed, 90.5 percent said that copyright education workshops are not required at their schools.

19. Renee Hobbs, Peter Jaszi, and Pat Aufderheide, *The Cost of Copyright Confusion for Media Literacy* (Washington, DC: American University, Center for Social Media, 2007).

20. According to my survey, librarians tend to see themselves as responsible for their schools' copyright questions (see appendix A).

CHAPTER 2
Lindsey's Copyright Is Infringed

A VERY GOOD PLACE TO START IS THE BEGINNING

In this chapter, I briefly focus on the history of U.S. copyright law and, more importantly, its policy implications. What is copyright intended to accomplish for the good of the public? In the early days of the new republic, what were the Founding Fathers thinking when they crafted copyright law? This section will be followed by a review of copyright law.

U.S. copyright law is derived from the British Statute of Anne (1710)—"An Act for the Encouragement of Learning"—and was further influenced by a landmark British court decision, *Donaldson v. Beckett* (1774), which made clear that copyright law was regulatory in nature and created by the government and not a "natural right" or perpetual right to control the publication of a work.[1]

Here is a short version of the story. In London, beginning in the sixteenth century, a series of licensing acts granted by the Crown governed the right to publish books. The government permitted the Stationers' Company—a group of publishers, printers, and booksellers in London—a perpetual monopoly. Because the Stationers' Company held the license to print an author's work in perpetuity, published works never fell into the public domain. In return, the company agreed to publish only those works that were sanctioned—that is, not censored—by the reigning monarch.[2] As time passed, the licensing acts continued to regulate the book trade even as suppression of speech became less of a concern. The monopoly status of the Stationers' Company remained in place and was thought to be an aid in controlling piracy.

The Statute of Anne abolished the monopoly and made significant changes to English copyright policy. The public interest purpose of copyright was defined—copyright encourages learning. As an incentive to create, authors (rather than members of the Stationers' Company) were granted copyright for a fourteen-year term and one renewal of fourteen years. Authors were required to register their works. Authors still sold their works to publishers, who continued to reap the majority of the economic rewards, but only authors were allowed to renew their copyright, which put a cap on the term of copyright and moved more works to the public domain. In spite of the law, booksellers continued to act as monopolists, justifying their actions by asserting that the Statute of Anne was merely a supplement to their natural right of perpetual monopoly.

The issue—whether copyright was a limited right created by the government or a natural law that was therefore perpetual and unconditional—was finally resolved by the House of Lords in the 1774 *Donaldson v. Beckett* decision. Donaldson was a Scottish publisher who sold reprints of old classics. Thomas Beckett was an author whose poem was reprinted by

Donaldson. Beckett, along with a group of English publishers, claimed that Donaldson was a pirate because Beckett's copyright was his common law property right and, therefore, absolute. In its ruling, the court reaffirmed that copyright law was a grant given to authors by statute. Authors did not *own* their creations in the same way they owned property or land. Instead they *held* the exclusive right granted by law to market their work for a limited time. Authors did not enjoy natural rights that extended throughout their lives as creators; copyright had a limit, and at the end of that term, works entered the public domain.

The Donaldson decision came late in the eighteenth century and was fresh in the minds of the American Founding Fathers. In 1783, before the formation of the federal government, the Continental Congress agreed that each colony should have a law to secure copyright for authors and encourage the dissemination of knowledge and creativity. Not surprisingly, the colonies that passed copyright law each retained the elements of the Statute of Anne—providing a grant of copyright to authors for their work that extended to a fourteen-year term with one fourteen-year renewal, after which works would enter the public domain. With the drafting of the Constitution a few years later, the Congress of the Confederation, recognizing the need for a uniform law across the country, gave the new Congress, in article I, section 8, the power to create a copyright law to, as we have seen, "promote the Progress of Science and useful Arts." The first federal copyright law was enacted in 1790.

The founders—intent on creating a government for the people and by the people—understood that without access to information, the public would not be up to the challenge of the new democracy. If the new country were to thrive, participation in the government by an informed citizenry was critical. Copyright was a law that would ensure that the public had access to information, because those who used their labor to create new knowledge, make new discoveries, or produce creative arts would have an incentive to disseminate their work by selling it and making it available to the public.

There's nothing like the satisfaction of completing a project or creating a new work. Knowing that you hold the copyright to the work heightens that feeling because the law has made it official. But in fact, copyright attaches to *any* new work at the point of creation, including the hundreds of little creations we produce every day. Writing the school a note excusing the absence of your sick child? Protected. Drawing doodles on your notepad during boring meetings? Protected. Videotaping the family vacation to the Grand Canyon? Protected. Copyright protects original and creative expressions "fixed in a tangible medium" at the point of creation, automatically. Next, we consider the scope of copyright: What does copyright protect? Who is the rights holder? What are the requirements for copyright? How long does copyright last? You get the picture.

COPYRIGHT NITTY-GRITTY

The Copyright Act of 1976 is the federal law that protects the creative expressions of authors, creators, artists, and other rights holders.[3] Congress grants "exclusive rights" to rights holders, who have the sole right to market their works. This monopoly over the sale of works is limited by numerous exceptions that allow others to use an exclusive right without prior

Glen Valley High School
569 Glen Valley Road
Hollingston, Wisconsin 53027-4237

Office of the Principal

MEMORANDUM

To: All Teaching Faculty, Librarians, and Staff
FROM: Kim Pickel
RE: Gary LeDuc's schedule at Glen Valley High

We are very fortunate that Gary LeDuc has extended his visit to meet with
staff that coordinate various school activities where copyright law issues
tend to crop up. Please make the most of these meetings by being prepared
ahead of time with your questions. For those who plan to join Mr. LeDuc for
lunch, please meet promptly at noon in my office, and we will walk over to
Bill Ho's.

November 2
9:30–10:30 Open time for individual appointments - Lindsey, Cliff
    (Staff Lounge)
10:30–12 Meeting with librarians (School Library Media Center)
12–1:30 Lunch at Bill Ho's Chinese Restaurant
2–3 Meeting with teaching faculty—Lena, Veronda (Staff Lounge)
3–4 Meeting with the school newspaper staff and students (Room 167)

November 3
10–12 Meeting on the Talent Show - open to all (Bentley Auditorium)
1–1:30 Wrap up and evaluation (Kim, Gary)

authorization from the rights holder. The statutory monopoly requires some constraints
to further the purpose of the copyright law—to advance learning and to protect freedom
of expression. For example, a book critic should be able to review a book without permission from the rights holder. This may involve quoting from the work to illustrate points or
critique. And because schools and libraries play a key role in the education of the public
and are therefore sites of learning, Congress provides some copyright restraints specifically
crafted for them. The policy objective of copyright law is to balance the interests of rights
holders with the rights of users of information.

Limited, Statutory Monopoly =
Exclusive Rights of Copyright

Rights holders have five exclusive rights (plus a sixth right applicable only to sound recordings) that constitute the monopoly over the sale of works:

(1) to reproduce the copyrighted work in copies or phonorecords;[4]

(2) to prepare derivative works based upon the copyrighted work;

(3) to distribute copies or phonorecords of the copyrighted work to the public by sale or other transfer of ownership, or by rental, lease, or lending;

(4) in the case of literary, musical, dramatic, and choreographic works, pantomimes, and motion pictures and other audiovisual works, to perform the copyrighted work publicly;

(5) in the case of literary, musical, dramatic, and choreographic works, pantomimes, and pictorial, graphic, or sculptural works, including the individual images of a motion picture or other audiovisual work, to display the copyrighted work publicly; and

(6) in the case of sound recordings, to perform the copyrighted work publicly by means of a digital audio transmission.[5]

Words Are Tricky

People frequently are confused by language that differs from the defined terms in the Copyright Act. The key is to figure out how the activity described by the language fits into the terms in the Copyright Act. The term "changing formats"—for example, transferring a videotape to the DVD format—is one of the most widespread examples of this. There is no exclusive right "to change format." Changing formats is an example of the reproduction right because the resulting DVD is a copy of the video—the content has not changed. Individuals often change the formats of materials that they own—as when they convert the digital audio files on a CD to MP3 or other format for use on another device. This is a personal use that is a reproduction, but because it is a fair use, it is not an infringement. In the library context, too, because of fair use and reproduction exceptions, some changes in formats would not be considered infringements.

The streaming of digital files is also often called an exclusive right, but it too is not in the Copyright Act. "Streaming" is in fact another way of "performing" a work. So is all streaming covered by the Copyright Act? Not necessarily. The exclusive right is for public performances, not all performances. So streaming infringes an exclusive right only if it involves streaming to the public. Likewise, the term "audio rights" may go beyond copyright's public performance right. A private performance, as of an audiobook played in the home or the car, is not covered by an exclusive right. Of course, these terms are used in license agreements all the time and may be enforceable as a matter of contract law. For example, there is no right "to access" a work, but libraries pay for access when purchasing digital resources for the library.

You Have a Package of Rights

Copyright amounts to a "bundle" of rights. And because this bundle is divisible, rights holders can manage one or more exclusive rights in numerous ways throughout the life of the copyright. Before you show a film to the public, you often have to get a license from the rights holder. In this case, the rights holder is allowing you the use of the right of public performance under nonexclusive conditions defined in the license. The nonexclusive condition of the contract allows the rights holder to sell his public performance right to others. The license may define additional restrictions that you must abide by—such as not advertising the title of the film in the local newspaper—unless you can negotiate terms. Licenses that appear to be straightforward and brief may harbor looming implications—as when an author inadvertently assigns exclusive rights to a journal publisher in perpetuity. In general, contract law takes precedence over copyright law, so you may license a database, for example, under use terms that are either more restrictive or more lenient than under copyright.

Initially, exclusive rights were limited to reproduction and distribution, but with the introduction of new formats and technologies, additional rights were added to account for the ways these formats are marketed and sold. For example, and at least initially, the public did not buy copies of motion pictures, because they had no way to "read" them at home. Instead, economic rewards were made by the sale of tickets to the exhibition or public performance of the films, thus the need for a public performance right. Today, we may buy DVDs of motion pictures, but the value of the work remains the performance.

HIGHLIGHT ON DERIVATIVE WORKS

The derivative work right applies to works that are based on the original—such as a translation. There can be all kinds of derivatives from a particular work: a game can be based on a film, or characters from the film can be represented by "action figures" that you get at McDonald's when you purchase a large Coke. Derivatives are based on the original, but they are separate works with their own copyright protection for any new creativity contributed by the second author. The original work is still protected separately with its complete set of exclusive rights. According to section 101 of the Copyright Act,

> A "derivative work" is a work based upon one or more preexisting works, such as a translation, musical arrangement, dramatization, fictionalization, motion picture version, sound recording, art reproduction, abridgement, condensation, or any other form in which a work may be recast, transformed, or adapted. A work consisting of editorial revisions, annotations, elaborations, or other modifications, which, as a whole, represent an original work of authorship, is a "derivative work."[6]

Some commentators argue that the derivative work right has expanded beyond what was originally intended by Congress. For example, in *Maljack Productions, Inc. v. UAV Corp.,* the copyright of the John Wayne film *McLintock!* had fallen into the public domain.[7] A producer—who happened to be John Wayne's son—took the original film, which was shot in Cinemascope, and reformatted it to fit on a then typical television screen using the "pan and scan" camera method. He also digitized the original sound track and registered the film as a new derivative work with the U.S. Copyright Office. Do these minor adjustments rise to a level of creativity that supports a new copyright? The court ruled that digitizing the original sound track did not add any new creativity to the original work but that the reformatted version of the film constituted a new work with its own copyright since the pan and scan process is not merely mechanical. As this example illustrates, one of the public policy implications of an expansive derivative work right is that fewer works will stay in the public domain (where they belong). Courts have ruled in other cases that the mere reproduction of a work in a new format does not represent a derivative work.[8]

PROTECTED WORKS

Works that are protected by copyright include everything from literary works to architectural works, but two things must be true. The work must be an *original* work with a degree of creativity, and it must be "fixed in a tangible medium"—perceptible to others in some fashion.[9] Fixation is a critical element of copyright public policy because it requires that works be perceptible in some form or reproduced in tangible copies that can be distributed to the public, thereby advancing the dissemination of information. If a work is original, created and fixed in a tangible medium, that work is immediately protected by copyright (no registration is required) for the copyright term of life of the author plus seventy years.[10]

THE TERM OF COPYRIGHT IS A LITTLE LESS THAN FOREVER

Congress has increased the term of copyright a number of times, eleven times in the last forty years. The Sonny Bono Copyright Term Extension Act of 1998 gave us our current term, up from life plus fifty years to life plus seventy. To determine how long a copyright lasts, add seventy years to the date that the author died. All terms of copyright go through the end of the calendar year (December 31).

Example: J. D. Salinger died in March 2010. His copyright continues to exist through the end of the year of his death—in this case, 2010—plus seventy years. The seventy-year count begins in 2011. Thus all of his works, including *The Catcher in the Rye*, will enter the public domain in 2081.

The original term of copyright was a mere fourteen years, with the option of one fourteen-year renewal if the author was still living. Copyright is a bargain we make with authors and other creators—a law that allows rights holders a limited, statutory monopoly in return for the creation and dissemination of their works to the public. The founders did not like the idea of sanctioning a monopoly, so they wished the term to be only as long as necessary to provide an economic incentive.[11]

After the term expires, a work enters the public domain, where anyone can make use of it—and even republish it. Hence, publishers can still make money selling the works of Shakespeare, Disney can make films based on fairy tales, and the Internet Archive can scan and post public domain works on the Web.

One rationale for increasing the term of copyright was the desire to put U.S. authors on a par with foreign authors, some of whom already had a "life plus seventy" term under their respective nations' laws. Copyright heirs who wanted to continue to capitalize on the works created by their relatives also desired a longer term. In fact, copyright heirs (as well as rights holders like Disney) went to Congress to ask for extensions to the copyright term so they could continue to collect royalties for works created by their grandparents. So, just as property, land, and possessions are passed down, copyright is passed on to heirs who played no role in the original creation of the work. Wouldn't it be great if your grandchildren continued to be paid your salary after your demise?

The public gains absolutely nothing by extending copyright duration.[12] Remember that the monopoly provided to authors was initially intended to motivate the creation and dissemination of creative works and discoveries to benefit the public. Clearly, if an author is dead, he can no longer create no matter how great the incentive. Some have argued that such a long copyright term is unconstitutional, but the Supreme Court ruled otherwise in *Eldred v. Ashcroft*.[13] The court ruled that Congress could make copyright term last as long as it felt was appropriate, just as long as it was not forever. One can anticipate that Congress will extend the term again (and again), a scenario that Peter Jaszi, professor of law at American University, famously dubbed "perpetual copyright on the installment plan."[14]

According to section 102 of the copyright law, protected works include

1. literary works
2. musical works, including any accompanying words
3. dramatic works, including any accompanying music
4. pantomimes and choreographic works
5. pictorial, graphic, and sculptural works
6. motion pictures and other audiovisual works
7. sound recordings
8. architectural works

NO PROTECTION FOR YOU!

Some materials are not protected by copyright law for critical public policy reasons. For instance, the law does not protect *facts*. Facts are different from creative expressions. Facts are discovered, not created. The free flow of facts is essential to knowledge building. If a fact could be "owned" by someone, you would have to ask permission every time you wanted to use the fact, or take the time necessary to rediscover the fact for yourself. It's difficult to conceive of a world where facts were not in the public domain.

A collection of facts (such as a bibliography) is not protected by copyright, but any creative aspects of the collection may be protected (as in an annotated bibliography). The *original selection and arrangement* of a collection of facts can also be protected by copyright. Most facts "live inside" of protected works. A textbook is a protected work, but it likely contains facts that are not protected. You can freely use the facts in any way, but you cannot freely use the protected elements of the textbook.

Federal *government documents* are not protected by copyright unless the material is written by a private entity hired by the government to create the work that retains copyright. It is in the public interest that citizens in a democratic society should have free access to the laws of the nation and the works of the government. This idea harkens back to the importance the founders placed on an informed citizenry, whose access to laws, court rulings, government agency reports, and so on, is critical to functioning successfully in a participatory democracy.

Other "unprotectables": lists, standard arrangements like the twelve-month calendar, processes (how to set the dining room table) and procedures (how to file your income taxes), some state documents when their governments do not claim protection. (You will find that more states are claiming copyright so that they sell state government documents to supplement their meager budgets.) In addition, no one can claim copyright protection for book titles or typeface designs or the verse form behind a sonnet or haiku.

IDEA VERSUS EXPRESSION DICHOTOMY

Copyright does not protect ideas, and for good reason. The free flow of ideas ensures open exchange of information and the ability to create new works from old ideas. Consider the idea for a television situation comedy about a family. There are many different expressions of this idea, from *I Love Lucy* to *Family Guy*. Consider the dominant plotlines of the soap opera genre—couples that break up and remarry repeatedly, characters trapped in hard-to-reach cabins during snowstorms, women delivering babies in places that are not the hospital (elevators, the backseats of cars, abandoned buildings, hard-to-reach cabins during snowstorms), and of course, paternity. These plotlines may be common in the soap opera genre, yet each time one occurs, it is expressed in a different way.

In *Walker v. Time Life Films*, Thomas Walker, author of a book called *Fort Apache*, brought an infringement suit against a movie company that made a film called *Fort Apache: The Bronx*.[15] Both the book and film dealt with the 41st Precinct in the South Bronx, which is commonly known as Fort Apache. Walker argued that the company, Time Life Films, infringed his copyright by basing their screenplay and subsequent film on his book. The court ruled for Time Life Films because, whereas the book and the film tell the same general story about police working in a dangerous district, each tell it in a different way. The book, on the one hand, is based on the real life of Walker as a police officer in the South Bronx. In the book, each chapter is a separate narrative based on actual events that Walker experienced as a police officer. The film, on the other hand, is one story that flows from beginning to end and includes several subplots with detailed characters that do not appear in the

The classic "idea versus expression" court case is the nineteenth-century Supreme Court ruling in *Baker v. Selden*.[16] Charles Selden wrote a book about bookkeeping and included a ledger similar to bookkeeping ledgers sold by W. C. M. Baker. The court spoke to two issues: Was Baker's bookkeeping ledger system—blanks forms with columns, lines, and headings—a protected work? And was it an infringement of copyright to explain the use of the ledger system as Selden did? The court ruled that the ledger system was such a basic design that it was not protected. It also said that anyone could write their own expression of how to use a bookkeeping system.

In the court's ruling, Justice Joseph P. Bradley wrote, "Where the truths of a science or the methods of an art are the common property of the whole world, any author has the right to express the one, or explain and use the other, in his own way."

book. For the court, the similarity ended with the basic story, or *idea*—the lives of police working in the South Bronx.

WHO HOLDS COPYRIGHT?

The creator or author of an original work holds the copyright to the work, but rights of copyright can be transferred.

(1) The ownership of a copyright may be transferred in whole or in part by any means of conveyance or by operation of law, and may be bequeathed by will or pass as personal property by the applicable laws of intestate succession.

(2) Any of the exclusive rights comprised in a copyright, including any subdivision of any of the rights specified by section 106, may be transferred as provided by clause (1) and owned separately. The owner of any particular exclusive right is entitled, to the extent of that right, to all of the protection and remedies accorded to the copyright owner by this title.[17]

Example: A researcher writes a paper that is later published in an academic journal. The researcher holds the copyright to his work but, under a contract with the publisher, transfers an exclusive right or more (the right of reproduction, the right of distribution) to the publisher. The publisher can then exercise an exclusive right that originally was held by the researcher to publish and sell the article to the public.

Note: Transfers of copyrights can be "exclusive" or "nonexclusive." An exclusive transfer means that only the one publisher (in the example above) is assigned those particular rights. Non-exclusive means that the rights holder may transfer the same right to other individuals or entities. Naturally, a publisher would negotiate for exclusive rights to eliminate any potential competitors.

Transfers of copyrights can also be time based. Say a librarian wants to establish movie night at the library. Showing movies to the public is a right held by the rights holder (in this case, the motion picture company). The librarian would—if the rights holder agreed—get a license for the right to publicly perform a work on the day of the movie screening only. This is also an example of a nonexclusive contract, because the rights holder can transfer the right to publicly perform to anyone as many times as desired.

A "work for hire" is one that is commissioned by an employer or other person. In a work for hire situation, the employer is hiring an individual to create a work for the employer under a written contract. The copyright is held by the employer unless the contract says otherwise.

> In the case of a work made for hire, the employer or other person for whom the work was prepared is considered the author for purposes of this title, and, unless the parties have expressly agreed otherwise in a written instrument signed by them, owns all of the rights comprised in the copyright.[18]

Who holds the copyright of works created by teachers and librarians? In general, when one creates works as a condition of their employment, the copyright holder is the employer, but this is different from a work for hire situation. As a school librarian or teacher, you create works all of the time—lesson plans, finding tools, and so on—fairly independently and without specific conditions established by the school. In other words, if you are developing a syllabus, the school in general does not tell you what to write, or how long or detailed the syllabus should be, and so on, as would be true in a work for hire situation. Nonetheless, you are being paid by the school to do a particular job, so the rights for materials you create are held by the school. The employer holds the copyright when you create the works during work time, using school resources and technology, and receive a regular paycheck with social security and insurance deductions. These conditions point to an extended and presumably ongoing relationship with your employer. In our opening scenario, Lindsey

> **Q:** If the school holds the copyright to your works, can you use those works outside of the school—at a conference or in a training session? Can you lend your lesson plans to other teachers in another district without asking for permission?
>
> **A:** The answer depends on how restrictive your school policy is about works created on the job. For the most part, members of an educational community tend to have a more open view about sharing works with colleagues because of their collective commitment to advance learning. In addition, unlike other creators, we do not make our living selling the works we create on the job. Many schools do not have a policy to address the ownership of librarian- and teacher-created content, something you may wish to pursue. Or you might let sleeping dogs lie: in forgoing a strict policy you will be free to determine the best course of action on a case-by-case basis. In many instances, use of works outside of the classroom will be fair uses.

believes that she holds the copyright to her recently completed lesson plan. But if she used school resources and created the lesson on "company time," the school likely holds the copyright.

WAYS TO FORFEIT RIGHTS

Some creators want their works to be used or distributed broadly, yet they are stuck with all of the copyrights that can curtail broad dissemination. There are ways to forfeit copyrights, and because copyright is a bundle of rights, individual rights can be surrendered separately or in any combination. If it is your intent to sacrifice all rights to anyone without your prior permission, you can declare that your work is in the public domain. Because copyright is automatic—the rule and not the exception—one must make it obvious that copyright does not apply by some easily discovered notation or declaration: "This work is in the public domain." Another option is to establish a license that declares what rights you want to relinquish. Using a Creative Commons (CC; www.creativecommons.org) license is one way of establishing a public record of your desires. Creative Commons licenses come in all kinds of forms, such as "Attribution for Noncommercial Use," which is symbolized by this designation:

This license means that you as the rights holder want to be recognized as the original author of the work, so any use of the work should be attributed to you, and that any non-commercial use (reproduction, distribution, public display or performance, the right to create derivative works based on the original work) is allowed. Many educational institutions place a CC license on their publicly accessible websites. The bonus is that if people want to use the work in the ways specified, one need not seek permission from the rights holder, saving everyone time and money. In addition, one has the option of placing a digital copy of the work on the Creative Commons website, where it can easily be found by others. The Creative Commons is a great place to go to find music, images, and photos that are free for use in educational and other settings.

PUBLISHED AND UNPUBLISHED WORKS

Published works are distributed in copies "to the public by sale or other transfer of ownership."[19] The draft of that journal article you have been meaning to finish is protected by copyright, but it is not published. Prior to the Copyright Act of 1976, unpublished works were not the subject of federal copyright law. Instead, state laws governed these works. Unpublished works are subject to the fair use exception, but courts have indicated that fair use may be narrower when a work is unpublished. In *Harper & Row v. Nation*, the Supreme Court ruled that the publication of a small portion from the manuscript of Gerald Ford's unpublished memoirs—in which he revealed his rationale for pardoning President Nixon—was not fair in part because Ford's opportunity for first publication was usurped, "scooping" a prominent element of the autobiography and thereby potentially affecting the market for the work.[20]

> Out-of-print works are still protected by copyright unless they are in the public domain.

 Q: What about creative works found on the Web? Are they protected? Are they published?

A: If a work meets the requirements of copyright—original, creative, and "fixed"—it is protected by copyright and all of the same rights and exceptions apply. The law suggests that if a creative work is publicly available for distribution, it is published: "The offering to distribute copies or phonorecords to a group of persons for purposes of further distribution, public performance, or public display, constitutes publication."[21] Thus far, however, courts have been divided on whether a public display of a website constitutes publication.

PLAGIARISM VERSUS INFRINGEMENT— DON'T CONFUSE THE TWO

Infringement is a violation of the copyright law. Plagiarism—passing off another's work as your own—is cheating, and *may* also be infringing if a court makes that determination. The distinction between the two is important, because some copying can be a fair use. The typical example is a student essay or research paper. The student may include portions of other works in her own work. This is a fair use. If the student cites those works in footnotes in her paper, she has not plagiarized—she is acknowledging that those specific portions are not her own work.

In the school setting, students are often encouraged to "copy" a work—particularly in the visual arts—in order to learn a skill or a technique. Trying to copy a drawing that looks exactly like the original is neither an infringement nor plagiarism because it is not a copy of the original. It is the creation of a new work, handmade and produced from scratch, and not an exact replica of the original. However, infringement and plagiarism do apply if one tries to pass off the new work as if it were the original and sell it in the marketplace. Clear as mud?

 Q: Does the use of citations protect a student from infringement?

A: No. A rights holder can sue anyone if he thinks that the use of the work is infringing. Of course, especially if the text used from the work is a small portion, this is highly unlikely.

BENEFITS OF REGISTRATION

Even though not required by law, formally registering your work with the U.S. Copyright Office has both public and personal benefits. If a work is registered, others that want to use the work can easily identify and locate the rights holder should permission be required. Registration is required prior to initiating an infringement suit, and if your work is registered within five years of its publication, you have proof in the court that you are indeed the rights holder.[22] If someone infringes your copyright, the fact that your work is registered demonstrates as false any claim by the infringer that he is the rights holder or that he could not have known the work was protected by copyright. And then of course, there's the money. If a work is registered, the rights holder is eligible to collect statutory damages if her copyright is infringed, as well as court and attorney's fees.

GOING TO COURT

Lindsey has a few options to consider if she really wants to sue a colleague for copyright infringement. The best option is to try to work the situation out with the alleged infringer before hiring a lawyer and heading to court. If Lindsey chooses to litigate, she faces a situation that would require a flowchart to illustrate.

- Think about what you really want out of the case. Do you want money? An apology? For the infringing work to be pulled? Start knowing what you want and thinking realistically about your chances of getting it.
- Try to work it out outside of court.
- Has it been more than three years since the last act of infringement? If so, the statute of limitations has tolled and you can't pursue federal claims. There are exceptions: for example, if the infringer intentionally concealed the infringement from you.
- Double-check: Do you really own the copyright? Or did you sign it away to a publisher or employer? If you do not own the rights, you must get the rights holder to sue.
- Make sure your work is registered. If it is not, register the work. (Be sure you have registered the actual work you claim has been infringed, not an earlier version. A later version is sometimes okay.)
- If your registration is rejected (e.g., the Copyright Office does not believe your work is an original), you must serve notice of your suit with the Register of Copyrights if you still intend to sue.
- Hire a lawyer. (If you have trouble finding a lawyer to take your case, it's a bad sign.)

- Think about your budget for the case. Your budget will determine how extensive trial preparation can be.
- Start saving all your records and find the ones that may be missing. This includes anything that might prove the material is yours and any proof that your colleague saw your work and copied it. A copyright suit requires (1) a copyrighted work and (2) infringement.
- Identify any parties that may be involved other than your colleague. Should an employer or publisher be named also?
- Send a cease and desist letter or demand letter to all parties.
- Send a preservation letter so they know to keep their records.
- Decide what remedies to ask for and put them in your complaint. Things you can ask for:
  1. destruction of the infringing material
  2. actual damages (your losses + infringer's profits) or statutory damages (determined by the court).

Note: If you registered within three months of your publication or anytime before the infringement started, you can ask for statutory damages or actual damages. You can also ask for attorney's fees. If you did not register within three months of publication or anytime before the infringement started, you can ask only for actual damages.

If you select actual damages, you will have to show factual justification for the amount.

Statutory damages are determined by the court and would depend on various issues. Was the infringement willful? Was the infringer completely unaware of having infringed? Statutory damages can range from $750 to $30,000 per infringement and can be raised to $150,000 per infringement. If the infringer was unaware, damages may be lowered to $200 per infringement.

- Think about any related claims you would like to include in the complaint; you won't be able to raise them in a separate suit.
- File a complaint in federal district court. (Not state court—copyright claims are litigated in federal court.) Serve the complaint and summons on defendant(s).
- Do you want a preliminary injunction? Move for one. There will be a hearing. Injunctions are granted when it can be shown that you will be harmed if the defendant's action is not stopped. You can ask that the defendant stop distributing; you can ask that all copies be impounded.
- Whether an injunction is granted or not, the case proceeds.
- The defendant can either file an answer to your complaint within the allotted period, file a motion (to dismiss, to strike, or for a more definite statement), or default (by not responding).
- Did the defendant default? File a motion for default judgment. Present your evidence to the court. You can be awarded a default judgment up to the amount you asked for in your complaint.

Copyright Infringement Decision Flowchart

Define your goals and consider options

Resolve out of court? — YES → END

NO

Has it been three years since the last act of infringement? — YES → Can you prove infringement was concealed? — NO → Statute of limitations: federal claims are barred

NO

YES

Continue court process → Is your work registered?

NO → Register your work

Are there other defendants?

YES

Consider secondary liability claims

Hire a lawyer ← YES

Examine your budget

Save your records

File your complaint

Did you register in a timely fashion or before infringement occurred? — NO → Ask for actual damages → Consider any related claims

YES → Ask for statutory damages and attorney fees

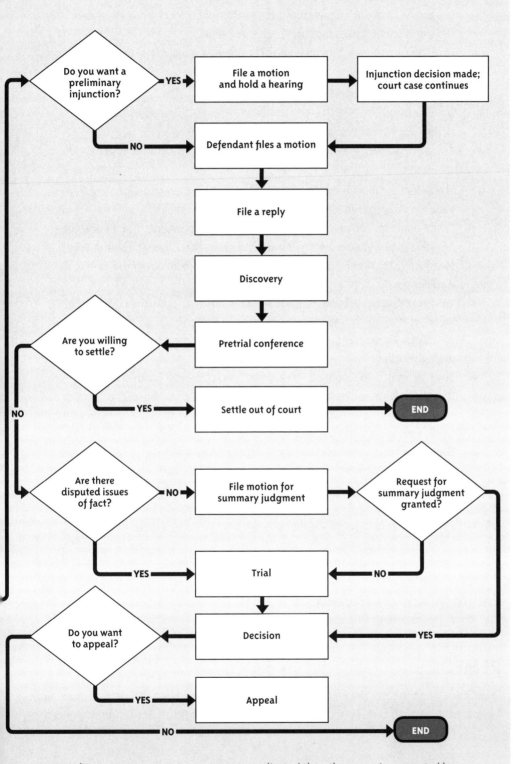

Note: Some infringement court cases are more complicated than the scenario presented here.

- Did the defendant counterclaim? Then you must also file a reply, and now you're in a mess of trouble because now you, too, are participating as a defendant.
- Did the defendant file a motion? You should reply.
- In response, was a defense claimed? The defendant may claim multiple defenses, including
    1. that you authorized the reproduction
    2. fair use
    3. independent invention
    4. invalidity (or "uncopyrightability"—e.g., you don't hold the copyright or copyright expired)

    The defendant must prove any such claim by a "preponderance of the evidence." Your reply should rebut them.
- Figure out what you need to win your case. What documents and other evidence are you missing? Request it from the other party. This is known as discovery. Meanwhile, the other party will be requesting documents from you to establish its defenses.
- You must disclose all your witnesses and exhibits at a pretrial conference, where you will also state the claims you will present at trial. You may amend pleadings. There may be an additional pretrial conference early on to form a discovery plan.
- You may want to negotiate a settlement. This is the most common exit plan—one that the judge may urge you to pursue. You can withdraw and settle at any previous time as well. The judge may also urge you to try arbitration or mediation—this is your last chance before trial begins.
- You may want to move for summary judgment. Usually this motion comes after discovery, when there are no serious factual disputes that would make or break a case. You can get a judgment if there is "no genuine issue as to any material fact." The defendant will almost certainly oppose. There will be a hearing.
- Finally, the court decides—either you get what you asked for or you don't, in which case you may want to appeal.

At any time during this entire course of events, you can move for withdrawal or dismissal of the case or choose to settle.

Whew. I think a short pause is in order.

REMEDIES

In an infringement case, the rights holder (or plaintiff) can elect the kind of monetary award she wishes to receive should the court rule in her favor. *Actual damages* is an award of all of the money the rights holder lost because of the infringement—such as royalty fees that were not collected. The rights holder also can collect any money that the infringer gained by the infringement. With actual damages, the amount of money awarded is based on some proof of lost revenue and illegal gains. Statutory damages are an amount established by the court—between $750 and $30,000—per work infringed. That's where the big money comes in. The Recording Industry Association of America, after winning infringement cases involving peer-to-peer file sharing, have been awarded huge sums—as much as $675,000 (or $22,500 per song infringed).[23] The award can go as high as $150,000 per work infringed if the plaintiff proves and the court finds that the infringement was "willful." A plaintiff has "willfully" infringed when he knowingly and recklessly disregards the law.

 Q: Can you be thrown in jail for copyright infringement?

A: Yes, it is possible under certain conditions. First, a federal prosecutor would have to convince the court that criminal penalties should be considered. The alleged infringer must have willfully infringed for commercial advantage or private financial gain and (a) made $1,000 worth of copies in a 180-day period or (b) infringed a work before it was commercially released.[24]

Now, are you scared half to death? Don't be. Criminal copyright infringement charges are rarely sought, approved by the court, and ultimately determined in court rulings. In civil cases, nonprofit libraries and educational institutions are protected from liability in a number of ways, as mentioned in chapter 1:

- by section 504 (remission of statutory damages for nonprofit educational institutions and libraries when the infringer believed his use was fair);
- by the Eleventh Amendment (protecting state entities from federal prosecution without consent); and
- by exceptions under the copyright law.

CONGRESS KNOWS BEST

Congress realized that libraries and educational institutions require more safeguards because they are centers of learning where the use of protected works is continual. As you will see in the two upcoming chapters, many exceptions to the law are allowed specifically for nonprofit libraries, educational institutions, and to a lesser extent, archives.

NOTES

1. An Act for the Encouragement of Learning, 1710, 8 Anne, c. 19 (Eng.); *Donaldson v. Beckett* (1774) 98 Eng. Rep. 257.

2. Throughout the sixteenth and seventeenth centuries, England was divided by those who supported Catholicism and those who followed the Church of England (early Anglicanism). The Stationers' Company agreed to censor those books that were in opposition to the reigning monarch's spiritual affiliation, as well as other writings critical of the Crown.

3. I use the term "rights holder" instead of "copyright owner" to illustrate that (1) copyright is not a property right, but rather an exclusive right provided by Congress, and (2) the rights of copyright can be transferred and held by someone other than the original creator.

4. "Phonorecords" is an old-fashioned word that still appears in the copyright law. 17 U.S.C. § 101: "'Phonorecords' are material objects in which sounds, other than those accompanying a motion picture or other audiovisual work, are fixed by any method now known or later developed, and from which the sounds can be perceived, reproduced, or otherwise communicated, either directly or with the aid of a machine or device. The term 'phonorecords' includes the material object in which the sounds are first fixed."

5. 17 U.S.C. § 106, "Exclusive rights in copyrighted works."

6. 17 U.S.C. § 101.

7. *Maljack Productions, Inc. v. UAV Corp.*, 964 F. Supp. 1416 (C.D. Cal. 1997).

8. See, for example, *Bridgeman Art Library v. Corel Corp.*, 36 F. Supp. 2d 191 (S.D.N.Y. 1999).

9. 17 U.S.C. § 102, "Subject matter of copyright: In general."

10. 17 U.S.C. § 302(a). And, according to § 302(c), if the work is anonymous, pseudonymous, or made for hire, the term of copyright is 95 years from its date of first publication or 120 years from the date of its creation, whichever comes first.

11. "The following [addition to the Bill of Rights] would have pleased me. . . . Monopolies may be allowed to persons for their own productions in literature and their own inventions in the arts, for a term not exceeding __ years but for no longer term and no other purpose." Thomas Jefferson to James Madison, August 28, 1789. ME 7:451, Papers 15:368.

12. "It is easy to understand how the statute might benefit the private financial interests of corporations or heirs who own existing copyrights. But I cannot find any constitutionally legitimate, copyright-related way in which the statute will benefit the public. Indeed, in respect to existing works, the serious public harm and the virtually nonexistent public benefit could not be more clear." Justice Breyer (dissenting), *Eldred v. Ashcroft*, 537 U.S. 186, 266 (2003).

13. *Eldred*, 537 U.S. 186 (2003).

14. *Copyright Term Extension Act of 1995: Hearing on S. 4839 before the Senate Judiciary Comm.*, 108th Cong. (1995) (statement of Professor Peter Jaszi, Washington College of Law, American University, September 20, 1995).

15. *Walker v. Time Life Films, Inc.*, 784 F.2d 44 (2d Cir. 1986).

16. *Baker v. Selden*, 101 U.S. 99 (1879).

17. 17 U.S.C. § 201(d).

18. 17 U.S.C. § 201(b).

19. 17 U.S.C. § 101.

20. Fewer than 400 words from former president Ford's 655-page typescript were quoted. *Harper & Row, Publishers, Inc. v. Nation Enterprises*, 471 U.S. 539 (1985).
21. 17 U.S.C. § 101.
22. 17 U.S.C. § 507(b) and § 507(a). The statute of limitations for copyright infringement is three years for civil cases and five years for criminal cases.
23. *Sony BMG Music Entertainment et al. v. Tenenbaum*, 672 F. Supp. 2d 217 (D. Mass. 2009). This award was later reduced to $67,500.
24. This criteria was added to the law with the No Electronic Theft (NET) Act of 1997.

CHAPTER 3
Kim Wants to Talk about Fair Use

This chapter focuses on the exceptions and limitations, including fair use, that provide balance to the rights holders' statutory monopoly. Exceptions and limitations allow users to exercise an exclusive right without prior authorization and without paying a license fee, under certain conditions. They are especially important for libraries and educational institutions—sites of learning—where copyrighted works are necessary for teaching and are the fodder for new creative work. We begin with fair use, because it is the exception that is most important for librarians and educators to understand and use.

FAIR USE—LOVE IT OR HATE IT

If copyright is difficult to grasp, fair use is the ultimate gray area of the law. Fair use relates to the unauthorized exercise of a copyright (such as the right to reproduce a work). If your use is fair, there is no need for prior authorization or payment to the rights holder. If you exercise fair use, and you are later sued for infringement, the fair use justification can be used as a defense in court. The court will determine whether your use is fair or infringing by evaluating your specific case using the four factors of fair use, as well as any other criteria deemed pertinent. In fact, fair use was created by judicial decisions made over time and later codified by Congress in the 1976 Copyright Act.

> [T]he fair use of a copyrighted work, including such use by reproduction in copies or phonorecords or by any other means specified by [section 106], for purposes such as criticism, comment, news reporting, teaching (including multiple copies for classroom use), scholarship, or research, is not an infringement of copyright. In determining whether the use made of a work in any particular case is a fair use the factors to be considered shall include—
> (1) the purpose and character of the use, including whether such use is of a commercial nature or is for nonprofit educational purposes;
> (2) the nature of the copyrighted work;
> (3) the amount and substantiality of the portion used in relation to the copyrighted work as a whole; and
> (4) the effect of the use upon the potential market for or value of the copyrighted work.

The fact that a work is unpublished shall not itself bar a finding of fair use if such finding is made upon consideration of all the above factors.[1]

In a decision from 1994, the Supreme Court observed that this text "employs the terms 'including' and 'such as' in the preamble paragraph to indicate the 'illustrative and not limitative' function of the examples given, . . . which thus provide only general guidance about the sorts of copying that courts and Congress most commonly had found to be fair uses. Nor may the four statutory factors be treated in isolation, one from another. All are to be explored, and the results weighed together, in light of the purposes of copyright."[2]

Fair use is abhorred by some because of its open-ended and context-sensitive nature. There are no yes or no answers; every fair use determination requires that one stop and think and, like judges, form an opinion. In the decision cited above, the Supreme Court cautioned that the process of determining fair use "is not to be simplified with bright-line rules, for the statute, like the doctrine it recognizes, calls for case-by-case analysis."[3]

But fair use is revered by others because its more general and flexible characteristics (compared to other copyright exceptions that are more regulatory in nature) adapt to a variety of situations, uses, and technologies. Fair use serves the public interest. It allows for the free flow of information. Without fair use, the copyright law would be overly rigid and our ability to learn, speak openly, criticize, and create new works would be stymied. Fair use is an "integral part of copyright, whose observance is necessary to meet the objectives of that law."[4]

Everyone—a student or teacher, a corporation, a motion picture company, a musician—draws on fair use when they are learning and creating. In a documentary called *John Lennon's Jukebox*, Lennon's private record collection illustrates the music that inspired him (Otis Redding, Wilson Pickett, the Lovin' Spoonful, among others).[5] We learn that riffs from some of the songs are mimicked in later Beatles recordings and that certain chord strings also are copied. This bor-

What was Congress thinking?? When you consider how dense and ambiguous fair use is, you may be wondering, "What genius came up with that one?" Here's what Congress was thinking:

The statement of the fair use doctrine in section 107 offers some guidance to users in determining when the principles of the doctrine apply. However, the endless variety of situations and combinations of circumstances that can rise in particular cases precludes the formulation of exact rules in the statute. The bill endorses the purpose and general scope of the judicial doctrine of fair use, but there is no disposition to freeze the doctrine in the statute, especially during a period of rapid technological change. Beyond a very broad statutory explanation of what fair use is and some of the criteria applicable to it, the courts must be free to adapt the doctrine to particular situations on a case-by-case basis. Section 107 is intended to restate the present judicial doctrine of fair use, not to change, narrow, or enlarge it in any way.[6]

"If I have seen further, it is by standing on the shoulders of giants." —Isaac Newton

rowing of works from others helped Lennon learn to be a musician and to create new music, which in turn led in part to new styles of rock and roll that other musicians emulated. All creators depend on the works of those who precede them. Thus many neighborhood garage bands owe a debt of gratitude to Deep Purple for that chord riff at the beginning of "Smoke on the Water."

THE FOUR FACTORS IN DEPTH

To consider whether a use of a copyright is fair, you must evaluate the four factors of fair use and then make a decision based on your best judgment. Ultimately, a use is fair when a court rules it to be so, so there is much to learn from fair use court decisions. Most of the decisions are not specific to libraries and schools (because there are few such cases), but you can glean how courts look at the four factors and apply that understanding to your own situation.

Each factor should be considered on a continuum, where on one end of the spectrum a factor is very clearly fair, and on the other end a factor is not fair at all. There is a middle area in the spectrum where many uses fall.

Depending on the situation, each factor will have a varying degree of significance. You will need to determine how strong a factor is as well as how important it is to your particular situation. All four factors should be considered, but in some instances one might not matter that much. It is unusual for all factors to be of equal significance. One or two will be more important than others.

Factor One: **Purpose of the Use**

Copyright's purpose is to advance learning by providing an incentive to creators of new works to make them available to the public. In educational settings, learning is a primary objective, so uses of works in educational settings are fairer than uses in noneducational settings. In particular, nonprofit educational uses are favored over for-profit, commercial uses because commercial uses can usurp the limited monopoly of the rights holder. Some uses, of course, fall somewhere in between the two extremes. And if uses by librarians and educators tend to be noncommercial in nature, this does not mean that all educational uses are fair, just as not all commercial uses are unfair. All four factors must be weighed. Other favored uses are those that "transform" the original work. These uses, which create something new and different from the original work, are described in more detail below.

Factor Two: **Nature of the Publication**

There are two aspects of the nature of the work used—whether it is unpublished or published and whether it is fictional or factual in nature. The use of an unpublished work can have a negative impact on a rights holder's ability to financially benefit from that work. If a work is

Q: The school plays portions of songs over the auditorium system, including popular music, during class breaks. Fair use?

A: Let's examine the four factors:

> The purpose of the use: In a nonprofit setting, the music is performed not for instructional purposes, but for background sound, potentially entertaining. This factor is in the middle of the factor one continuum. The purpose is not for profit, but it's not for educational purposes either.
> The nature of work being used: Music is considered highly creative and therefore deserving of more copyright protection, suggesting that the nature factor is not fair.
> The amount of work performed: Only portions of the songs are played, suggesting that the use is more likely fair.
> The effect on the market for the work: All of the music has been previously purchased, indicating a minimal effect on the market for the work. Some might suggest that the performances could enhance future sales of the works to students.

> Determination: This use is fair with factor four—effect on the market—an important consideration because the music has been purchased. Another aspect of this use that influences our fair use determination is that the use is fairly innocuous. One should consider the harmlessness of the alleged infringement. In addition, playing music in the morning (perhaps with morning announcements) or in between classes is common—an indication that the use has been accepted as normal and is *tolerated*.[7] Rights holders may be aware of these uses but choose not to care about them because their use is inconsequential or is an aid in publicizing their works.

copied and exposed to the public prior to its publication, why would anyone buy the work? Works that are fictional in nature also have a stronger copyright protection layer. These works are considered more creative, and their use may be tied to entertainment or pleasure, whereas a factual scholarly journal article is more likely tied to learning. In a very simplistic explanation, factual works should be more broadly disseminated while fictional works—with their greater emphasis on creativity, a requirement for copyright protection—should have less exposure because they have a thicker layer of copyright. If you intend to parody another work, however, the creative nature of the original will carry less weight in your analysis.[8]

Factor Three: **Amount Used**

Small portions are favored over larger chunks, but this factor is not solely quantitative. Using a short portion that is considered to be the "heart" of the work may not be considered fair. From a quantitative point of view, the amount must be considered in the context of the use. Using an entire work may be fair if it is the only way your purpose can be achieved.

Q: Most student and staff copying is unsupervised—for example, no one monitors what copies students are making at the photocopier, and students often print out copies of articles they find on library databases or elsewhere on the Internet. Should the school establish rules to ensure that copyright is not abused?

A: No. Unless one knows otherwise, assume that the students and staff are copying materials for learning, research, and study purposes. Making personal copies for individual learning is an exemplar of fair use. To remind students and staff that unreasonable levels of copying may be infringing, label photocopy equipment and computer terminals with signs that provide a warning about copyright law.[9]

From a qualitative perspective, evidence indicates that taking the heart of the work, especially in the context of a commercial purpose, is rarely deemed fair.[10]

Factor Four: **Effect on the Market for the Work**

With this factor, one must consider the detrimental impact an unauthorized use of a work may have on the market for the work. If the work is obscure, or not commercially viable or available, unauthorized use has less of an impact. Downloading a current Hollywood film and distributing the file on the Internet, on the other hand, would have a greater impact. One must also consider viable and likely revenue streams that financially benefit the rights holder, such as royalty markets—a flow of revenue collected via permission fees. However, the existence of a royalty market does not mean that the use is automatically unfair. The fourth factor is on par with the other three factors and should not be given primacy. As the Supreme Court explained "the importance of this factor will vary, not only with the amount of harm, but also with the relative strength of the showing on the other factors."[11]

A WORD ABOUT FAIR USE GUIDELINES

Fair use "guidelines" are rules designed to quantify fair use. Instead of considering the reasons why some copying or other use of an exclusive right is not an infringement of copyright but rather a fair use, such guidelines are based almost entirely on the *amount* of copying allowed. Guidelines have been developed by stakeholder groups to establish a common understanding of the interests of all—a worthy goal, but a shortsighted policy position.

Many of these guidelines have not been endorsed by library associations because they are so specific that there is the fear that they will tie down the options users of information

From: Kim Pickel <kim@glenvalley.miles.k-12.wi.us>
Sent: Tue 10:16 AM CST
Subject: **Drinks?**
To: Lola Lola <lola@wessex.edu>

Lola:

Are you free for a cocktail this week? If we go to Café Dahlia, we won't have to shout to hear ourselves speak. How about Thursday, right after work?

I want to talk to you about LeDuc's presentation. What did you think? He didn't mention fair use at all which I thought was strange. I want the staff to respect the copyright law, but they should also realize that there are user rights as well. I'd love to hear your opinion.

Best,
Kim

_____

Kim Pickel
Principal
Glen Valley High School
Go Grizzlies!

have in using copyrighted works in lawful ways. Nonetheless, many libraries follow specific guidelines even though they do not appear in the statute and do not have the force and effect of the copyright law.

When Congress created the fair use exception, its intention was *not to quantify fair use*. Congress feared that fair use, reduced to numbers and percentages, would not be flexible enough to account for the various ways people might use copyrighted works in the future. Nonetheless, publishers, authors, and eventually some librarians wanted more certainty. They formed a stakeholder group to develop what became the "Agreement on Guidelines for Classroom Copying in Not-for-Profit Educational Institutions with Respect to Books and Periodicals," which was read into the House Report on the Copyright Act of 1976. The House Committee on the Judiciary, while making it clear that the guidelines did not take the place of fair use, nonetheless believed that they were "a reasonable interpretation of the *minimum* standards of fair use."[12]

The preliminary paragraphs of the classroom copying guidelines read as follows:

> The purpose of the following guidelines is to state the minimum and not the maximum standards of educational fair use under [section 107]. The parties agree that the conditions determining the extent of permissible copying for educational purposes may change in the future; that certain types of copying permitted under these guidelines may not be permissible in the future; and conversely that in the future other types of copying not permitted under these guidelines may be permissible under revised guidelines.

> Moreover, the following statement of guidelines is not intended to limit the types of copying permitted under the standards of fair use under judicial decision and which are stated in [section 107]. There may be instances in which copying which does not fall within the guidelines stated below may nonetheless be permitted under the criteria of fair use.[13]

Over the years, a number of fair use guidelines have been developed for music, multimedia, e-reserves, off-air broadcasting, and other kinds of copying conducted for educational purposes.

Most of the library associations suggest that adhering to guidelines is not in the long-term interests of users of information. Once you establish a set of numbers and percentages, those numbers become maximums, and a ceiling on fair use is established. It is ridiculous to think that copying 10 percent of anything is fair but copying 11 percent is an infringement. Courts have found that copying less than 10 percent is infringing. Likewise, sometimes copying an entire work is fair, depending on the circumstances. A desire for the easy answer leads us to blindly follow hard-and-fast rules that have no legal basis. Many people justify the use of guidelines because fair use is "too nebulous" for students and staff to understand. Don't sell your school community short. As you will see in this book, most of the activities that students and teachers engage in are reasonable uses of protected works, conducted as part of the learning and creating process, which is spontaneous and circuitous. When you learn, teach, or create, you cannot plan your path of discovery and creativity with a checklist of percentages in mind. Librarians support open inquiry, access, and use of information—indeed, these are the values that the library profession is based on. Needless to say, there are some uses that are infringing, and I will identify some throughout the book.

To reiterate:

- Fair use guidelines are arbitrary rules that authors, publishers, librarians, and others have developed as a way of quantifying fair uses.
- They are not in the copyright law.
- They were initially considered minimum standards of fair use, meaning that going over a stated guideline (such as copying more than 10 percent of a book) may also be fair, but have since been practiced as maximums.
- Using percentages to determine lawful copying is not compatible with the open-ended, creative process of learning, researching, and creating new works.
- Fair use is more about having a reasonable diet and less about counting calories.

A SPECIAL NOTE ON INTERLIBRARY LOAN GUIDELINES

During the drafting of the Copyright Act of 1976, controversy arose among stakeholders regarding reprographic equipment—photocopiers as well as emerging computer technologies. Congress, in order to move forward with the legislation, chose to set aside these issues until further study could be conducted. The National Commission on New Technological Uses of Copyrighted Works (CONTU) was given three years to study and make legislative and procedural recommendations on

(1) the reproduction and use of copyrighted works of authorship—

    (A) in conjunction with automatic systems capable of storing, processing, retrieving, and transferring information, and

    (B) by various forms of machine reproduction, not including reproduction by and at the request of instructors for use in face-to-face teaching activities; and

(2) the creation of new works by the application or intervention of such automatic systems of machine reproduction.[14]

In terms of interlibrary loan, the commission addressed several questions: Was there a need to create a mechanism for collecting royalties for interlibrary loan copying? How much did it cost for libraries to subscribe to and maintain journal collections? Was it more efficient to fulfill interlibrary loan requests by making copies of articles or by borrowing bound journals from other libraries? What was the volume and nature of existing photocopying activities conducted in libraries for interlibrary loan purposes? Two studies were conducted, and the commission concluded that there was no need to change section 107 (fair use) or section 108(g) (photocopying by libraries for interlibrary loan purposes) and that current interlibrary loan practices did not warrant additional regulation. However, the commission did create the CONTU interlibrary loan guidelines.

The CONTU guidelines deserve separate mention not only because substantial thought and deliberation took place when they were developed, including the use of research data but also because the CONTU guidelines are practiced in libraries to such a wide extent that they have become a norm. Perhaps this is due to the fact that interlibrary loan operations break down into a specific workflow, a series of steps taken to meet a user request. If your library conducts a lot of interlibrary loan lending and borrowing, efficient workflow is a necessity. In addition, student assistants are often hired to do much of the interlibrary loan grunt work. The need to train new students semester after semester correlates with a need to have established workflow patterns that provide consistency of service.

The CONTU guidelines, reprinted in appendix F, are not without controversy. While they have worked fairly successfully for libraries, rights holders have been less enamored. In the digital environment, rights holders want to move to a pay-per-article market, effectively eliminating a lot of the article sharing that now occurs. On the other hand, many researchers and journal authors are making their works more readily available, often free of charge in digital repositories and open-access publications.

TRANSFORMATIVE USES

Legal scholars have noted a recent tendency in copyright cases. Courts have placed more emphasis on the first fair use factor—purpose of the use.[15] Transformative uses of works—secondary uses that are innovative, add value, produce new meaning, or repurpose or recontextualize the original work—advance the purpose of copyright law by furthering the creation of new expression in ways that are socially beneficial. According to Judge Pierre Leval, these secondary uses add value and create new insights and are "the very type of

activity that the fair use doctrine intends to protect for the enrichment of society.'"[16] This trend to focus on the purpose of the use is a positive development, not only because most educational uses are not-for-profit but because many educational uses are transformative. I will highlight a few examples below.

Parody and Satire

With parody and satire, an author mimics or otherwise transforms a creative work for the purpose of commenting on or criticizing some aspect of the work. In *Campbell v. Acuff-Rose Music, Inc.*, the Supreme Court ruled that 2 Live Crew exercised fair use when the band produced a parody version of the Ray Orbison classic "Pretty Woman" as a commentary on life on the urban streets.[17] In *Blanch v. Koons*, the Second Circuit noted that use of a portion of a photograph as raw material for a collage was transformational. In this case, an artist copied a part of a magazine ad for Gucci sandals featuring a pair of women's legs and included it in his painting, which satirized mass media's profound effect on society. In both of these cases, the courts ruled that the uses were fair even though they were of a commercial nature.[18]

New Uses

When a new function or utility is created by using existing works, courts also have ruled that these uses are fair. For example, Google, Yahoo, and other search engines essentially copy entire websites without permission, but they do so in order to create searching capacity (an index), a highly transformative and beneficial use that serves the public interest.

In *Perfect 10 v. Amazon.com*, a U.S. Court of Appeals found "a search engine may be more transformative than a parody, because a search engine provides an entirely new use for the original work, while a parody typically has the same entertainment purpose as the original work."[19]

In a case argued in Virginia and later affirmed by the Fourth Circuit, the fair use doctrine was invoked as justification for its ruling that Turnitin's Internet plagiarism database was transformative. Even though Turnitin scanned and archived entire student papers for a commercial purpose, the court ruled fair use.

> Plaintiffs originally created and produced their works for the purpose of education and creative expression. iParadigms, through Turnitin, uses the papers for an entirely different purpose, namely, to prevent plagiarism and protect the students' written works from plagiarism. iParadigms achieves this by archiving the students' works as digital code and makes no use of any work's particular expressive or creative content beyond the limited use of comparison with other works. Though iParadigms makes a profit in providing this service to educational institutions, its use of the student works adds "a further purpose or different character" to the works, and provides a substantial public benefit through the network of educational institutions using Turnitin. Thus, in this case, the first factor favors a finding of fair use.[20]

Repurposing and Recontextualizing

Another category of transformative uses is repurposing. This involves the use of a protected work in ways that were not initially intended. For example, an educator teaching media literacy may use a variety of resources from popular media—including advertisements, feature films, and YouTube videos—as examples of "how to read" popular culture. Making copies of these works for this pedagogical reason transforms the original purpose of the work, making the use more likely fair. According to Jonathan Band, "Under this view of fair use, when a teacher reproduces a poem, a sound recording, or a photograph so that his students can study the work, his use is transformative."[21] Many uses of copyrighted works made by students can be considered repurposed uses, as long as the use is not a "substitute for creative effort."[22] In *Bill Graham Archives v. Dorling Kindersley*, the Second Circuit ruled in favor of the defendant, who without prior authorization included copies of Grateful Dead concert posters in her book detailing the history of the band. The court said that the use of the posters was "plainly different from the original purpose for which they were created" and that the images served as "historical artifacts to document and represent the actual occurrence of Grateful Dead concert events" in the book's featured timeline.[23]

Q: Students can choose to make a video or write a ten-page paper for their final assignment in their Race and Gender Studies class. Many of the students create videos and, naturally, include content from other videos to include in their own productions. Is this a transformative use?

A: Yes, because the students are using content from other sources not for the original purpose intended but to make new meaning. Let's say one student decides to copy clips from a series of television shows to depict the stereotypical treatment of Native Americans in popular media. This is a use of the original works that was not initially intended. (Of course, the student should cite each resource used.)

Other examples of transformative fair uses in the K–12 environment:

- A teacher assigns a project where students are asked to create a sound track of popular songs in which the lyrics relate to a particular topic of study. The students must justify their choices and cite the sources. (The resulting sound track is a mix of existing works, but the students have gathered these resources to learn about a topic.)

- A teacher copies and compiles photographs, images, charts, graphs, maps, and so on, and presents them as PowerPoint slides or on SmartBooks for instructional purposes.
- A teacher copies a number of poems for distribution in the classroom; students are asked to compare poetic styles.
- Students choose to create a parody of a TV show; this would require using enough aspects of the original work to ensure the class can understand what is being parodied.
- A school exhibit mixes a variety of protected works to tell a story about a topic.
- A school library develops pathfinders or indexes to certain works and posts them on the school website. These may include copies of book covers to direct students to the work held in the library.
- To prepare students for the state graduation test, a teacher copies practice tests and posts them to a secure website.

This chapter focused on the concept of fair use and its importance in balancing an overly strict copyright law, and demonstrated that many instances of fair use in the educational setting are transformative. This is especially true in our current environment, where students and others make meaning through the use of various media.

FIVE THINGS YOU SHOULD KNOW ABOUT FAIR USE

1. Fair use is your primary tool for making copyright decisions because it can address the myriad of copyright situations not addressed specifically in the copyright law.
2. Fair use guidelines are not the law, but they are frequently used to control the copying behavior of students and teachers and to manage workflows.
3. All four factors of fair use should be considered when making a fair use determination, but it is likely that one or two factors will be more important than the others, depending on the situation at hand.
4. Transformative uses—when works are used in a different way than originally intended to create new meaning or functionality—are favored as fair uses.
5. Some uses of protected works have reached the status of "tolerated." These are uses so widely practiced that they are considered lawful.

NOTES

1. 17 U.S.C. § 107.
2. *Campbell v. Acuff-Rose Music, Inc.*, 510 U.S. 569, 577–78 (1994).
3. *Id.* at 577.
4. Pierre N. Leval, "Toward a Fair Use Standard," *Harvard Law Review* 103, no. 5 (March 1990): 1105.
5. *John Lennon's Jukebox.* PBS Great Performances, Educational Broadcasting System.
6. H.R. Rep. No. 94-1476, at 66.

7. For more on tolerated uses see Tim Wu, "Tolerated Use," Columbia Law and Economics Working Paper No. 333 (May 2008), http://ssrn.com/abstract=1132247.

8. *Campbell*, 510 U.S. at 586.

9. See appendixes B, E, and F for more information.

10. Barton Beebe, "An Empirical Study of U.S. Copyright Fair Use Opinions, 1978–2005," *University of Pennsylvania Law Review* 156, no. 3 (January 2008): 616.

11. *Campbell*, 510 U.S. at 590.

12. H.R. Rep. No. 94-1476, at 72 (1976). My italics.

13. *Id.* at 68.

14. Library of Congress, *Final Report of the National Commission on New Technological Uses of Copyrighted Works* (CONTU) (Washington, DC: U.S. Government Printing Office, 1979), 8–9.

15. Jonathan Band, *Educational Fair Use Today*, Association of Research Libraries, December 2007, www.arl.org/bm~doc/educationalfairusetoday.pdf; Pat Aufderheide and Peter Jaszi, *Recut, Reframe, Recycle: Quoting Copyrighted Material in User-Generated Video*, American University, Center for Social Media, January 2008, http://aladinrc.wrlc.org/bitstream/1961/4604/1/CSM_Recut_Reframe_Recycle_report .pdf; Michael J. Madison, "Some Optimism about Fair Use and Copyright Law," *Journal of the Copyright Society of the U.S.A.* 57, no. 3 (2010), http://ssrn.com/abstract=1619916.

16. Leval, "Fair Use Standard," 1111.

17. *Campbell*.

18. *Blanch v. Koons*, 467 F.3d 244 (2d Cir. 2006).

19. *Perfect 10, Inc. v. Amazon.com, Inc.*, 487 F.3d 701, 721 (9th Cir. 2007).

20. *A.V. et al. v. iParadigms, LLC*, 544 F. Supp. 2d 473, 482 (E.D. Va. 2008).

21. Band, *Educational Fair Use Today*.

22. American University, Center for Social Media, "Code of Best Practices in Fair Use for Media Literacy Education," [2010], www.centerforsocialmedia.org/fair-use/related-materials/codes/code-best -practices-fair-use-media-literacy-education.

23. *Bill Graham Archives v. Dorling Kindersley*, 448 F.3d 605, 609 (2d Cir. 2006).

CHAPTER 4
The School Media Center Is Renovated

LIBRARY AND EDUCATION-RELATED EXCEPTIONS

Including fair use, the U.S. copyright law has fifteen exceptions and limitations, but only a few are generally used by libraries and schools. These exceptions are more specific than fair use—in some cases, they are more like checklists, where certain things must be true for the exception to apply. However, they have no impact on the fair use exception, which can always be considered when using a protected work. For example, the Copyright Act contains a specific exception for libraries to make a reproduction for purposes of replacing a damaged or lost copy. Under this exception, digital copies must remain on the premises of the library. However, after conducting a fair use analysis, the library might decide to allow access to the digital copy outside of the library's premises.

Library Reproductions

This is the exception that everyone loves to hate because it is inflexible—and out of date.[1] Nonetheless, the exception has its high points, particularly in regard to copies made for interlibrary loan. It was written with the photocopy machine in mind, so when we make reproductions in digital formats, fair use will generally guide us rather than this exception.

This exception allows for reproductions made for preservation and replacement purposes, by library users, and for interlibrary loan as long as the following is true:

(1) the reproduction or distribution is made without any purpose of direct or indirect commercial advantage;

(2) the collections of the library or archives are (i) open to the public, or (ii) available not only to researchers affiliated with the library or archives or with the institution of which it is a part, but also to other persons doing research in a specialized field; and

(3) the reproduction or distribution of the work includes a notice of copyright that appears on the copy or phonorecord that is reproduced under the provisions of this section, or includes a legend stating that the work may be protected by copyright if no such notice can be found on the copy or phonorecord that is reproduced under the provisions of this section.[2]

The Specta

"Home of the Grizzlies"

Volume XIX Issue 3

L to R: Teacher Veronda Taylor, Patrick Monahan, 9th grade, Librarian Lindsey Eagen Hancock, Principal Kim Pickel, Head Librarian Lena Valez, Superintendent Dr. Mark Boschle, Maggie Chin, 10th grade

Grand Opening of Library Celebrated

On October 27th, Principal Kim Pickel welcomed students, teachers, parents, and library friends to the grand opening of the new Glen Valley High School library media center. School superintendent Dr. Mark Boschle was also on hand to thank members of the community for the continued support of the library renovation project supported by a bond obligation (Proposition 8) passed by the citizens of Miles County. Dr. Boschle praised the community for its foresight in understanding that a state-of-the-art media center was a key ingredient of student academic success. "Without a media center of the highest caliber, we cannot teach today's students—digital natives who learn in new ways because digital technology has always been a part of their lives." Dr. Boschle also thanked the Bond Obligation Implementation Team for their leadership and perseverance in seeing the renovation to completion. "The team's true dedication and unfailing optimism in spite of setbacks made this dream a reality."

The architectural firm OEP Associates was also on hand for the festivities and praised the staying power of the library and technical support staff. "They were all extremely patient and cooperative even through the two-week phase of loud drilling. Glen Valley is lucky to have such dedicated staff," said lead architect Samuel Oppenheim.

The library media center, nearly the size of four regular classrooms, boasts a new 32-computer technology lab, an information desk, traditional book storage and display, as well as a high-tech media production center and group study rooms. A segmented vault skylight in the center of the library is eye-catching. Students were "blown away" by the new center. Tenth-grader Michaela Drew commented, "The new library media center is fantastic. The space is so cool, students will want to hang out here." Patrick Monahan, 9th-grader, was impressed by the media production center. "The media production center is sweet. I'll definitely be in there making videos."

Preserving Unpublished Works or Replacing Published Works

These exceptions—sections 108(b) and (c)—allow the library to make up to three copies of a work for preservation or replacement purposes. A special distinction is made between unpublished and published works. Under the law, you can make a *preservation or security copy* of an unpublished work, and you can *replace* a published work.

 Tip: Section 108 does not authorize you to make copies of published works to hold in an archive *in case* the original is damaged or stolen.

Preservation:

(b) The rights of reproduction and distribution under this section apply to three copies or phonorecords of an unpublished work duplicated solely for purposes of preservation and security or for deposit for research use in another library or archives . . . if—

(1) the copy or phonorecord reproduced is currently in the collections of the library or archives; and

(2) any such copy or phonorecord that is reproduced in digital format is not otherwise distributed in that format and is not made available to the public in that format outside the premises of the library or archives.

 Q: If I make a replacement copy of a published work in a digital format, can I loan the new copy?

A: This is an aspect of section 108 that is troublesome. If you are making a replacement copy, you probably want to use it in the same way as the original copy, but the law indicates otherwise. Why? Rights holders are concerned that a digital file made accessible outside of the library is a risky proposition because of the ease of making and distributing near-perfect copies. In practice, libraries do loan and borrow digital works that are in tangible formats—like a CD—just as they would loan a book. This is a regular practice and not infringing. Nonetheless, because CDs and DVDs can be replicated quite easily, take the extra step and label these formats with a copyright warning statement. If the replacement copy exists only as a digital file on the library's network, a fair use determination may indicate that lending the file is allowed. It would be wise to establish extra security mechanisms for digital files protected by copyright. Perhaps you could provide access to the file only to the user who requests the work and establish a password gateway.

Q: The school district has discarded our VHS machines and has moved to a DVD-only format. Does the copyright law allow us to make DVD copies of all of our VHS tapes? We have a small budget and cannot afford to buy replacement copies for the entire video collection.

A: Under Section 108, if a DVD copy is available for purchase to replace a VHS tape, you must buy the DVD replacement copy. For those titles that you cannot purchase, after making a reasonable search for an unused copy, you can make a replacement copy in the format of your choice (assuming that VHS machines are no longer manufactured or reasonably available in the commercial marketplace).

Q: How do you make a replacement copy from a copy that is damaged or stolen?

A: Obtain a copy from another library.

Q: We have old filmstrips that we want to copy onto PowerPoint slides. Can we?

A: Yes, if the filmstrips are not available for purchase in the desired format. Because the filmstrip format is obsolete, you do not have to wait until the filmstrips are damaged or stolen.

Q: If we make a replacement copy, can we use that copy to circulate?

A: Yes. When you replace a work, which may be in another format if all of the above conditions are met, the assumption is that you no longer retain the old copy. The one copy that you made can be circulated just as the original copy you used to have, unless the new copy is a digital copy (but see next Q&A). Then you cannot circulate it. Clear as mud?

Q: Suppose I have one CD missing from a twelve-CD set? The distributor will only sell a complete set and does not offer a replacement price for just the one CD.

A: In this situation, the single CD is not available in the market for a reasonable price, so making a copy without authorization from the rights holder is justified.

Replacement:

    (c)   The right of reproduction under this section applies to three copies or phonorecords of a published work duplicated solely for the purpose of replacement of a copy or phonorecord that is damaged, deteriorating, lost, or stolen, or if the existing format in which the work is stored has become obsolete, if—

        (1)   the library or archives has, after a reasonable effort, determined that an unused replacement cannot be obtained at a fair price; and

        (2)   any such copy or phonorecord that is reproduced in digital format is not made available to the public in that format outside the premises of the library or archives in lawful possession of such copy.

An obsolete format is one for which the "playback" equipment is no longer being manufactured or is not readily available in the market.

Digital Copies

What in the world is Cliff doing? Making copies of hundreds of titles without rights holder permission? This can't possibly be legal.

Cliff's desire to make digital copies in this way is not addressed by section 108, but don't stop there. Always consider fair use, because the use might be lawful given the situation at hand. A fair use analysis can also help identify other solutions or ways to make the use "more fair." In this situation, the titles will be reproduced, but there is also an expectation that they will be publicly performed in the classroom. As we will learn in chapter 5, classroom performances are exempt. Assuming that nonprofit educational institutions are allowed to show lawfully acquired audiovisual works in the face-to-face classroom, the question remains: can you make a copy of a work in order to show it in class?

> Factor One: The purpose of these digital copies is to facilitate a nonprofit educational use. If access to the server is protected, only teachers can access the works, ensuring that the digital copies will be used only for instructional purposes. This factor weighs in favor of fair use.
> Factor Two: Depending on the work, this factor might tilt toward or against fair use. For a feature film with little educational value, this factor weighs against fair use. For a news show taped from a broadcast, this factor weighs in favor of fair use.
> Factor Three: Entire videotapes and DVDs will be copied. Is it necessary to copy the entire work? This factor seems to weigh against fair use, but how do the teachers plan to use the works? Do they need to show entire films? This factor may require further investigation.
> Factor Four: Is there an effect on the market for the work? If there is no available license for making server copies and then streaming the work, then there is no impact on the market. Moreover, because the library has already purchased a lawful copy and has a right to perform that work under section 110(1), perhaps the library would never have purchased a license to make the server copies.

A straight counting of factors doesn't clearly favor—or disfavor—fair use. What do you do then? Remember that certain factors often carry greater weight than other factors. Factor one—the purpose of the use—seems to be very important to our analysis, but it can be made even stronger. I would suggest digitizing those titles only when and if they are requested for teaching. In this way, wholesale copying of an entire collection is avoided—why make copies that may never be used? This strengthens the fair use argument because digitization is conducted only when the need—a nonprofit educational use—presents itself.

Reproductions for Library Users and Interlibrary Loan

Section 108 parts (d) and (e) allow librarians to make copies at the request of library users.

> (d) The rights of reproduction and distribution under this section apply to a copy, made from the collection of a library or archives where the user makes his or her request or from that of another library or archives, of no more than one article or other contribution to a copyrighted collection or periodical issue, or to a copy or phonorecord of a small part of any other copyrighted work, if—

(1) the copy or phonorecord becomes the property of the user, and the library or archives has had no notice that the copy or phonorecord would be used for any purpose other than private study, scholarship, or research; and

(2) the library or archives displays prominently, at the place where orders are accepted, and includes on its order form, a warning of copyright in accordance with requirements that the Register of Copyrights shall prescribe by regulation.

Plain language: Copying a small portion of a work for a library user is allowed when the copy is for personal use only. You can even distribute a copy to a user at a different library (interlibrary loan).

(e) The rights of reproduction and distribution under this section apply to the entire work, or to a substantial part of it, made from the collection of a library or archives where the user makes his or her request or from that of another library or archives, if the library or archives has first determined, on the basis of a reasonable investigation, that a copy or phonorecord of the copyrighted work cannot be obtained at a fair price, if—

(1) the copy or phonorecord becomes the property of the user, and the library or archives has had no notice that the copy or phonorecord would be used for any purpose other than private study, scholarship, or research; and

(2) the library or archives displays prominently, at the place where orders are accepted, and includes on its order form, a warning of copyright in accordance with requirements that the Register of Copyrights shall prescribe by regulation.

Plain language: Libraries can copy an entire work or a large portion of a work for a library user if a copy of that work cannot be purchased and the copy is for personal use only.

Section 108(f) gives some important reminders about reproductions made by libraries including liability protection.

(f) Nothing in this section—

(1) shall be construed to impose liability for copyright infringement upon a library or archives or its employees for the unsupervised use of reproducing equipment located on its premises: Provided, That such equipment displays a notice that the making of a copy may be subject to the copyright law;

Plain language: Section 108 does not mean that a library is liable for the infringing acts of library users making copies on a publicly available photocopy machine as long as a warning of copyright is placed on or near the photocopy machine.

(2) excuses a person who uses such reproducing equipment or who requests a copy or phonorecord under subsection (d) from liability for copyright infringement for any such act, or for any later use of such copy or phonorecord, if it exceeds fair use as provided by section 107;

Plain language: Section 108 does not excuse a library user who uses the library photocopier to make copies in excess of fair use or uses copies obtained from the library in a way that exceeds fair use.

(3) shall be construed to limit the reproduction and distribution by lending of a limited number of copies and excerpts by a library or archives of an audiovisual news program, subject to clauses (1), (2), and (3) of subsection (a); or

(4) in any way affects the right of fair use as provided by section 107, or any contractual obligations assumed at any time by the library or archives when it obtained a copy or phonorecord of a work in its collections.

Plain language: Section 108 neither enlarges nor restricts fair use. Licenses take precedence over the exceptions in section 108 (and can include terms that expand or restrict users' rights under section 108).

When librarians are making reproductions for any purpose, section 108(g) offers some important things to take into consideration:

(g) The rights of reproduction and distribution under this section extend to the isolated and unrelated reproduction or distribution of a single copy or phonorecord of the same material on separate occasions, but do not extend to cases where the library or archives, or its employee—

(1) is aware or has substantial reason to believe that it is engaging in the related or concerted reproduction or distribution of multiple copies or phonorecords of the same material, whether made on one occasion or over a period of time, and whether intended for aggregate use by one or more individuals or for separate use by the individual members of a group; or

(2) engages in the systematic reproduction or distribution of single or multiple copies or phonorecords of material described in subsection (d): Provided, That nothing in this clause prevents a library or archives from participating in interlibrary arrangements that do not have, as their purpose or effect, that the library or archives receiving such copies or phonorecords for distribution does so in such aggregate quantities as to substitute for a subscription to or purchase of such work.

Plain language: The library is not a full-blown copy shop, making copies willy-nilly. Reproductions are made only when necessary. Reproductions are not made to avoid the purchase of works at other libraries. Interlibrary loan should be reasonable.

Code of Federal Regulations, Title 37, Section 201.14, Warnings of copyright for use by certain libraries and archives.

(a) Definitions.

    (1) A *Display Warning of Copyright* is a notice under paragraphs (d)(2) and (e) (2) of section 108 of title 17 of the United States Code as amended by Pub. L. 94-553. As required by those sections the "Display Warning of Copyright" is to be displayed at the place where orders for copies or phonorecords are accepted by certain libraries and archives.

    (2) An *Order Warning of Copyright* is a notice under paragraphs (d)(2) and (e) (2) of section 108 of title 17 of the United States Code as amended by Pub. L. 94-553. As required by those sections the "Order Warning of Copyright" is to be included on printed forms supplied by certain libraries and archives and used by their patrons for ordering copies or phonorecords.

(b) Contents. A Display Warning of Copyright and an Order Warning of Copyright shall consist of a verbatim reproduction of the following notice, printed in such size and form and displayed in such manner as to comply with paragraph (c) of this section:

    NOTICE WARNING CONCERNING COPYRIGHT RESTRICTIONS

    The copyright law of the United States (title 17, United States Code) governs the making of photocopies or other reproductions of copyrighted material.

    Under certain conditions specified in the law, libraries and archives are authorized to furnish a photocopy or other reproduction. One of these specific conditions is that the photocopy or reproduction is not to be "used for any purpose other than private study, scholarship, or research." If a user makes a request for, or later uses, a photocopy or reproduction for purposes in excess of "fair use," that user may be liable for copyright infringement.

    This institution reserves the right to refuse to accept a copying order if, in its judgment, fulfillment of the order would involve violation of copyright law.

(c) Form and manner of use.

    (1) A Display Warning of Copyright shall be printed on heavy paper or other durable material in type at least 18 points in size, and shall be displayed prominently, in such manner and location as to be clearly visible, legible, and comprehensible to a casual observer within the immediate vicinity of the place where orders are accepted.

    (2) An Order Warning of Copyright shall be printed within a box located prominently on the order form itself, either on the front side of the form or immediately adjacent to the space calling for the name or signature of the person using the form. The notice shall be printed in type size no smaller than that used predominantly throughout the form, and in no case shall the type size be smaller than 8 points. The notice shall be printed in such manner as to be clearly legible, comprehensible, and readily apparent to a casual reader of the form.[3]

Reproductions in the Last Twenty Years of Copyright Term

There is a new exception for reproductions (which is rarely used) that was added to the copyright law, as section 108(h), when the Digital Millennium Copyright Act was passed in 1998:

(h) (1) For purposes of this section, during the last 20 years of any term of copyright of a published work, a library or archives, including a nonprofit educational institution that functions as such, may reproduce, distribute, display, or perform in facsimile or digital form a copy or phonorecord of such work, or portions thereof, for purposes of preservation, scholarship, or research, if such library or archives has first determined, on the basis of a reasonable investigation, that none of the conditions set forth in subparagraphs (A), (B), and (C) of paragraph (2) apply.

(2) No reproduction, distribution, display, or performance is authorized under this subsection if—

(A) the work is subject to normal commercial exploitation;

(B) a copy or phonorecord of the work can be obtained at a reasonable price; or

(C) the copyright owner or its agent provides notice pursuant to regulations promulgated by the Register of Copyrights that either of the conditions set forth in subparagraphs (A) and (B) applies.

(3) The exemption provided in this subsection does not apply to any subsequent uses by users other than such library or archives.

As you can see, section 108 is pretty wordy and can be confusing. You can find a helpful tool for mastering section 108 at the Copyright Advisory Network.[4]

Making Copies for Educational Purposes

Teachers frequently want to make copies of journal articles or other works to distribute in class. Section 108 does not address this kind of copying, so each time a teacher wants to make copies and distribute them, a fair use analysis should be conducted. That sounds like a whole lot of work, but consider that, as an example of fair use in section 107, Congress included "multiple copies for classroom use." Of course, copying can go beyond fair use, and permission may be required. It will be a judgment call that you and your institution must make. For example, the law gives no guidance on when or if a fair use, conducted repeatedly, becomes infringing. Your practice should reflect what you believe is reasonable given the situation and your risk tolerance.

A similar conundrum presents itself when teachers want to make reading packets in lieu of a textbook as the required class reading. A market for course packs is well established, and in general, these regularly copied articles and other readings should be used with the rights holders' prior permission.[5] However, remember to first make a fair use determination for each work in the packet before seeking permission. There may be instances when permission is not required—for example, if the work is in the public domain, if only a small portion of an entire work is used, or if the nature of the work is entirely factual, as in the case of a weights and measures chart. Other considerations might include whether the library has an ongoing subscription to the work (as for a periodical). To avoid such questions, educators should consider including open-access materials or materials publicizing that they can be used for nonprofit educational purposes, such as many of the resources found at the Creative Commons.

Consumables

The urge to make copies of workbooks or other materials that are meant to be "used up" by each student can be tempting, but copying these consumables clearly has a negative impact on the market for the work. Workbooks, test guides, and other consumables depend on a market where many copies are sold, one for each student. Occasionally, educators may purchase curriculum resources or other teaching guides that can be copied. A notation on such a publication may read "This guide may be photocopied for free distribution without restriction" or "Permission is granted to individual teachers to reproduce this guide for classroom use only."

Placing Digital Copies on Course Websites

Educators may maintain class websites where they post readings for the class. If the course website is password protected and only enrolled students have access to the materials, the use may be fair unless there is a clear attempt to avoid purchase of the work. There are no definitive copyright rules for course websites, so your judgment (again) has to come into play. Consider if there are other ways to give students access to the materials—for example, by placing a copy on reserve in the library. It may not be as convenient, but you are less likely to have to seek permission and pay a royalty fee for materials that are used every school year.

FIRST SALE

The free lending of their collections is a central feature of most libraries. Most of us assume that this is what libraries are for, but did you know that it would be a copyright infringement

---

Q: Is it okay for students to make copies of articles in periodicals or to print out or save articles found on the Web?

A: This is an example of making a personal copy. If you display a copyright warning sign at the sites where copies can be made, and assuming that the copy is made for personal study or educational purposes only, the exception at section 108(e) (reproduction for library users) comes into play, indicating that these uses are not infringing.

if not for the "first sale" doctrine? First sale allows libraries that have legally obtained a copy of a copyrighted work the right to lend, rent, sell, or otherwise dispose of that particular copy.[6] In other words, the copyright law says that an owner of a copy can distribute that copy without the authorization of the rights holder. Once a library buys a book, it can lend that copy to a student or another school through interlibrary loan. If you own some old LPs you want to sell to a used record store, you can do so. You can destroy or throw out those old ¾-inch videotapes your husband is saving (for some reason) without telling the rights holder that you are going to do so. It is your choice if you tell your husband.

The first sale doctrine has an important public policy function. To increase the dissemination of information, tangible copies can be shared and enjoy a "second life" with another person. Some creative works go out of print, but we still have those previously purchased copies we can hunt down at the library, buy on eBay, or preserve for coming generations.

A license agreement can limit the first sale doctrine, particularly with digital resources. For example, textbook publishers do not get any of the revenue collected from used book sales (a fact they find very annoying), but they could sell you a textbook as an e-book with license terms that restrict your right to resell the e-book.

Software

If a library wants to lend computer software that it owns, it can do so unless the software is purchased under a license agreement that restricts such use.[7] If you lend software, you must label the copy with the following warning:

> **NOTICE: WARNING OF COPYRIGHT RESTRICTIONS**
> The copyright law of the United States (title 17, United States Code) governs the reproduction, distribution, adaptation, public performance, and public display of copyrighted material.
>
> Under certain conditions specified in law, nonprofit libraries are authorized to lend, lease, or rent copies of computer programs to patrons on a nonprofit basis and for nonprofit purposes. Any person who makes an unauthorized copy or adaptation of the computer program, or redistributes the loan copy, or publicly performs or displays the computer program, except as permitted by title 17 of the United States Code, may be liable for copyright infringement.
>
> This institution reserves the right to refuse to fulfill a loan request if, in its judgment, fulfillment of the request would lead to violation of the copyright law.[8]

Tip: The library owns other such materials that may be easily copied. Write an abbreviated version of this copyright warning and make and place labels on these materials as a reminder to students about copyright.

Adding Gifts to the Collection

When a librarian sees some nice person coming into the library with a box of surplus books, she may want to run for cover. People just don't realize that giving the library their unwanted collection takes decision-making and processing time. Sometimes the materials are "gifts" that you would never want to receive or even consider for the library collection. Why can't these folks just give the library some money instead? Or vote yes on a tax referendum to support education? But sometimes you find a gem.

The first sale doctrine allows a person with lawful copies the right to give those copies away to anyone, including the library, but can the library always accept these gifts? When is a copy a *lawful* copy, and what if you do not know?

A lawful copy is one that has been acquired in the marketplace, even a secondary marketplace like a used bookstore. Oftentimes, educators receive complimentary copies of new titles from publishers who want to publicize their availability to their anticipated customer base. These books may be labeled in ways that restrict your right to give the book away. It usually is not a copyright infringement for a person who receives an unsolicited complimentary copy with such a restrictive label to sell the copy or give it away. Nonetheless, the library probably should not accept these books as gifts to add to the collection. At academic institutions, a faculty member may offer her own copies of journals to the libraries so the library can avoid paying for an institutional subscription. Again, this is an ethical issue more than a copyright concern.

Some people donate CDs, DVDs, and other formats that are easy to copy to the library. If it is clear that the items are personal copies of musical recordings or of television, cable, or other video programs (rather than purchased copies), you should not accept them.

Lending Equipment Along with Content

A relatively new practice is the lending of e-readers or iPods already loaded with content. If you buy a CD and then load the content onto an iPod, you own the content, so the iPod can be loaned. There is a complication when the content is acquired through a license agreement. Let's say you purchase several songs from iTunes and load them onto an iPod. In order to purchase those songs, you agree to a "terms of use" contract—in fact, you cannot purchase songs from iTunes until you have agreed to the contract. When reading the contract, you will discover that the content is sold to you for "personal, noncommercial purposes only." This language seems to indicate that libraries cannot use the content, much less loan the content. Nonetheless, libraries are doing just that.

Teachers may ask students to purchase songs from iTunes as part of their class materials, and this seems more acceptable because students will use the content individually, for private study. One might question whether the purchased music can be played aloud in class—again, not a commercial use but not a personal use either. There are a lot of questions about whether downloaded content can be used by libraries and in schools without violating the terms of use. Unfortunately, so-called click-on or click-through terms of use contracts (see chapter 6) may be legally binding and are frequently more restrictive than copyright law. Thus far, even though libraries and schools may be violating contracts, most of them go ahead anyway. Meanwhile, there has been no outcry from the sellers of devices or the rights holders of the content. In fact, we may see vendors providing contract terms that are more library-friendly, something many e-book distributors who recognize the extent of the educational and library market have done.

SUMMARY

There are five things you should know about library reproductions of protected works and the first sale doctrine:

- The copyright law provides specific exceptions that allow nonprofit libraries to make copies without prior authorization
    for library users
    for interlibrary loan
    for preservation and replacement
- Most instances of copying by libraries depend on a fair use evaluation and are not covered by section 108.
- Making digital copies is limited under section 108 but may be possible under fair use.
- When making copies for classroom use, fair use is your guide.
- The first sale doctrine allows libraries (and others) the right to lend, rent, sell, or dispose of lawfully acquired copies.

NOTES

1. 17 U.S.C. § 108, "Limitation on exclusive rights: Reproduction by libraries and archives."
2. 17 U.S.C. § 108(a).
3. 37 C.F.R. 201.14.
4. Section 108 spinner, http://librarycopyright.net/108spinner/.
5. The Copyright Clearance Center is the primary clearinghouse collecting royalties for course packs.
6. 17 U.S.C. § 109, "Limitations on exclusive rights: Effect of transfer of particular copy or phonorecord."
7. 17 U.S.C. § 109(B)(2)(A).
8. 37 C.F.R. 201.24.

CHAPTER 5
Patrick Inserts a Video Clip

"Digital native" is a term coined by Marc Prensky in his 2001 article "Digital Natives, Digital Immigrants" to describe people who were born after digital computing had become ubiquitous.[1] These "natives" grew up with digital technologies, while those of us who were born earlier and remember things like the typewriter are "digital immigrants"—people who adopted digital technology a little later in life. Prensky's thesis is that students who are digital natives, having always known computers, cell phones, and video games, think and learn in a different way from predigital people. They are fluent in the language of information technology, so naturally the ways that they choose to communicate tend to involve digital technologies.

Students increasingly mix text, images, video, and music in their class assignments, and of course, most of this material is protected by copyright. Copyright infractions can be kept to a minimum if teachers set clear parameters for classroom assignments, learn to recognize when students plagiarize or do not provide enough original content, and promote the use of citations. In general, when students use media and text in ways that transform the original works—that is, in ways that are different from what was originally intended, in order to create a new work or new function—they are exercising fair use.

Because educators play a significant role in helping digital natives to be good digital citizens, we have valid concerns about the importance of students understanding the copyright law. The sky is not the limit, yet it is generally fair use and not an infringement when students copy protected works and toss them into an assignment.

If copying is wrong, how can some copying be good?

This is a quandary I have heard frequently from school librarians and educators, and I think the answer lies, again, in understanding the purpose of the copyright law and conveying this to your school community.

- The purpose of the copyright law is to promote learning and the dissemination of knowledge to benefit the public.
- Learning and creativity do not occur in a vacuum. One needs access to existing knowledge to create new knowledge.
- Thus the use of original works in new works is allowed under the law in some cases, particularly in educational settings.
- But in order to have access to this knowledge, the public has made a bargain with creators and rights holders.

- This bargain is a limited, statutory monopoly. Rights holders have a monopoly over the sale of their creations with critical statutory limits, such as fair use.
- Fair use allows for the use of works without prior permission in order to advance new learning and urge the creation of new works, such as works that students create.

However, fair use is not unlimited. We exercise fair use with care by using only the amount of a work that we need and by providing full citations to acknowledge original authorship and to signal our own recognition that these works are not our own creations.

Fair use is more limited outside of the educational environment, so what was fair at school may not be fair in other settings, particularly commercial venues.

Q: Some students want to submit their works to competitions or distribute their works more broadly outside of class. What are the copyright implications if they have included other copyright-protected works as a matter of fair use?

A: Because fair use determinations are situation dependent, if the situation changes, the fair use determination will likely change. For example, if a student submits a video to a competition, the purpose of the use is no longer educational. If the student wins a monetary award, the situation now has economic implications. If the video is posted on a publicly accessible website, the work is no longer contained within the educational environment and has been widely distributed. Thus if a student (or a teacher!) wants to use his work outside of class, the fair use analysis should be conducted all over again.

PUBLIC PERFORMANCE AND DISPLAY

Section 110 is the exception to the exclusive rights of public performance and public display—in other words, when you can exercise the rights of public performance and display without the authorization of the rights holder. This is another detailed section of the law, but for our purposes we will focus on only two subsections—performances and displays in the face-to-face classroom and those in the digital distance or blended classroom (where online technologies and digital materials are used in conjunction with traditional face-to-face teaching).

First, the relevant definitions:

> To "display" a work means to show a copy of it, either directly or by means of a film, slide, television image, or any other device or process or, in the case of a motion picture or other audiovisual work, to show individual images nonsequentially. . . .

To "perform" a work means to recite, render, play, dance, or act it, either directly or by means of any device or process or, in the case of a motion picture or other audiovisual work, to show its images in any sequence or to make the sounds accompanying it audible.[2]

Think of *display* as a showing of art slides, one by one, in a classroom. Think of *perform* in terms of a theatrical performance or motion picture type media, including television.

It is not an infringement of copyright to display or perform a work *privately*. You can watch television, sing in the shower, or hang a photograph in your office without the rights holders' permission. According to section 110,

To perform or display a work "publicly" means—

(1) to perform or display it at a place open to the public or at any place where a substantial number of persons outside of a normal circle of a family and its social acquaintances is gathered; or

(2) to transmit or otherwise communicate a performance or display of the work to a place specified by clause (1) or to the public, by means of any device or process, whether the members of the public capable of receiving the performance or display receive it in the same place or in separate places and at the same time or at different times.[3]

Section 110(1) of the copyright law provides an exception for the display or the performance of a work "by instructors or pupils in the course of face-to-face teaching activities of a nonprofit educational institution, [or] in a classroom or similar place devoted to instruction." Thus showing a motion picture in DVD format for educational purposes in a classroom without the copyright owner's permission is lawful, so long as the motion picture has been lawfully acquired. Once a DVD is purchased, it can be shown in class without also having to purchase a public performance license. Similarly, a teacher can read a children's book aloud and display the illustrations to her class.

Tiered Pricing

Some distributors will sell DVDs at tiered pricing levels, with a lower price for individuals and a higher price for institutions such as schools. They may say that you have to pay the

 Q: Does this mean you do not have to pay the higher institutional price for a DVD?

A: The answer depends on why the higher institutional price is charged. Does the higher price allow for free or low-cost replacement copies? Do you get accompanying educational materials with the purchase? Or do you think the higher fee is justified because, ultimately, many people at the school will see the DVD? These may be reasons to pay the higher fee.

higher price in order to obtain public performance rights. But you do not have to purchase public performance rights if you intend to show the title only in class. If you plan to show it in a film festival or for entertainment purposes, a public performance license is necessary because those performances are not exempt.

Public Performance Licenses

A complication (there's always a complication!) to the section 110(1) exception occurs if the distributor doesn't sell copies but just licenses them, and the license prohibits public performances, including classroom uses. In that situation, the distributor might be able to charge extra for the public performance right. In other words, by calling a transaction a license rather than a sale, the vendor might be able to circumvent the section 110(1) exception Congress gave to educational institutions. Unfortunately, more distributors are taking advantage of this trick to charge higher prices to libraries and educational institutions.

Public performance licenses can be obtained at the point of acquisition. In this way, the public performance right is obtained for an indefinite amount of time. Some distributors may refer to this as "life of the video." You have a public performance right as long as the video survives. If you want to obtain a second copy of the work, you have to pay for the public performance license again.

Another way to obtain a license is to contact a distributor or subdistributor when you want to conduct a public performance. In this instance, you agree to a license with the distributor to publicly perform the work for that performance alone. This is common practice for film series exhibitions, where the title is only going to be shown once.

A final way to obtain public performance rights is to sign a license agreement and pay an annual fee to a company such as Movie Licensing USA that represents many film studios. This is a blanket license that allows for public performances throughout the term of the contract. Blanket licenses are usually limited to feature films. Educational films or documentaries are generally handled individually with the film distributors or rights holders.

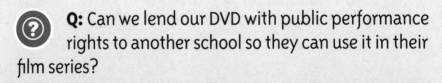

Q: Can we lend our DVD with public performance rights to another school so they can use it in their film series?

A: No. The public performance rights do not attach to the DVD—they attach to the licensee of the DVD—your school. You cannot transfer your license to another school.

Home Use Only

Can you buy a DVD at Walmart and show it in the classroom even though the film is labeled "home use only"? Yes, educators working in nonprofit educational institutions benefit from the copyright exception that allows for public performance in the classroom. The labeling on the item or language that appears at the beginning of the film does not apply. Notices like "No copying allowed" are inaccurate because fair use or specific exceptions like the ones in section 110 may apply. However, if the teacher rents the DVD from Netflix, the rental agreement may prohibit all public performances, including classroom uses that otherwise would be permitted under section 110(1).

If the library acquires a gift of feature-length DVDs, can the films be shown in the classroom? Yes. Assuming that the DVDs have been obtained lawfully, the exception applies to the nonprofit educational institution that is making the use, not to the person who originally purchased the work.

The Family Home Movie Act

In *CleanFlicks v. Soderbergh et al.*, several motion picture directors, including Steven Soderbergh, together with several motion picture companies, sued CleanFlicks for copyright infringement. CleanFlicks was a company that purchased DVDs or obtained them from its customers, edited them by removing "sex, nudity, profanity and gory violence," and then sold the edited copy to individuals and film rental vendors. In order to edit the DVD, they disabled its Content Scrambling System—the encryption technology employed by the rights holders. Each time someone requested a CleanFlicks film, the company bought another copy of the original DVD, in hopes of legally justifying any copyright infringement.[4]

The motion picture companies did not sell expurgated versions of their films directly to consumers, but they did make them available to the airlines for in-flight viewing. The directors, as "auteurs," opposed the practice because their works were being manipulated and changed in ways they never intended. The plaintiffs also argued that their rights to create derivative works as well as their reproduction and distribution rights were infringed. The defendants argued that their use was fair and—albeit for commercial purposes—provided a valuable service to families sick and tired of smutty movies.

While the court case was going on, Congress heard an earful from consumers who valued the CleanFlicks service. The result was the Family Home Movie Act of 2005,[5] which amended section 110 to allow the editing of motion pictures by a member of a private household, for private performance, as long as no altered version is fixed (and as long as the editing is limited to skipping over or eliminating "limited portions of audio or video content"). The amendment also allows for the creation and distribution of software or other technology that enables a member of a private household to engage in such editing. What? Congress wiggled out a policy that made almost everyone happy—fixed copies of altered films were not allowed, but consumers could buy and use filtering technology to edit the motion pictures *as they played on the DVD player*. The only loser was CleanFlicks, whose fair use argument did not stand up in court.

But what does this have to do with schools that cannot or do not want to show R-rated films?

You guessed it!! Fair use!

In response to the claim that a school infringes the right to prepare derivative works, the school has a strong fair use argument for using the same filtering technology to edit films as they play for classroom purposes. The use is nonprofit and educational, the DVDs are lawfully acquired, and full film viewing is already accepted in section 110(1). An added bonus is the fact that the school board has directed the schools to take such action based on the school community's principles.

The Technology, Education, and Copyright Harmonization (TEACH) Act

The TEACH Act of 2002 amended section 110(2) to allow for the digital transmission of copyright-protected content for nonprofit, educational purposes. The law sought to recognize that distance education was on a par with face-to-face classroom instruction and so should enjoy the same copyright exceptions. But because digital content is easier to copy and further distribute, rights holders wanted measures included in the law to temper the possibility that digital content would be infringed. The result was a more complicated law that is more restrictive than plain old section 110(1).

Several prerequisites must be in place before the educational institution can exercise these new exceptions.

The performance or display must occur "under the actual supervision of an instructor as an integral part of a class session offered as a regular part of the systematic mediated instructional activities of a governmental body or an accredited nonprofit educational institution." And it must be "directly related and of material assistance to the teaching content."[6]

Technical measures must be used to limit access to students enrolled in the course or government employees as part of their official duties, to prevent retention of the work for longer than the class session, and to prevent further dissemination of the work. Any such technological protection measures used by the rights holder must not be tampered with.[7]

There are some additional limitations:

- The educational institution must have a copyright policy in place and provide copyright education materials to teachers, students, and relevant staff.
- Only limited portions of most films, television, stage plays, and other media with a dramatic element can be *performed* via digital networks in the classroom.
- The amount of any work that is *displayed* should be comparable to the amount that would be displayed in a face-to-face classroom session.[8]

What is allowed or not allowed under the TEACH Act continues to be a controversial topic. TEACH can be interpreted in strict or more lenient ways. As a result, educational institutions have developed varying practices. At this time, we have no court rulings to help us better understand how to interpret TEACH.

Fortunately, *the fair use doctrine is not affected by TEACH*, so educators can use the four factors of fair use to determine if the use and transmission of digital content for educational purposes is fair instead of relying on the TEACH Act. While there is no guarantee that all digital transmissions of protected works are fair, if the content can be limited to educational use, the fair use argument is more convincing. It is therefore wise to borrow an idea from TEACH—use password protection to limit access to course materials to enrolled students only. Place a copyright warning statement on protected content as a reminder to teachers and students that the materials must not be copied or distributed.

Probably the most controversial element of the TEACH Act is whether or not an *entire* film can be transmitted for digital education purposes. A close reading of section 110(2) would indicate that only "reasonable and limited portions" can be used. Under a fair use assessment, the screening of an entire film is often justifiable. Some vendors are now selling "streaming rights" to higher educational institutions as a digital public performance right that would sanction the screening of entire films via digital transmission. This is an example of breaking down an exclusive right into several parts—one public performance license for screening in the analog environment, another public performance license for the very same screening but in the digital environment—allowing the rights holder to sell an exclusive right more than one time. In a license agreement, this is completely legit. Librarians rarely challenge such license terms, believing that it's "just the way the market is," thus establishing new buying behavior.

But some believe that paying an additional fee for a performance right that one already has is not necessary. If Congress wanted to eliminate the distinction between the face-to-face classroom and the digital classroom, why don't we have the same exception in both situations? Answer: Motion picture industry lobbyists successfully convinced Congress that excusing digital public performances for educational purposes would create great market harm. To further complicate matters, new vendors have entered the scene, offering to store and stream digital content for educational institutions. It is not clear whether these vendors—which are not accredited nonprofit educational institutions but rather for-profit companies—can stream content without infringing copyright, unless they have prior permission from the rights holders. On the other hand, using a streaming service is very convenient for educational institutions who do not want to bother with servers and other IT issues, so why not pay someone else to provide that assistance? But if you do so, are you paying for the service or are you paying for the public performance right? In many respects, the TEACH Act remains a puzzle that many educational institutions choose to ignore altogether, confident in relying on fair use as an alternative.

Making Compilations

Say a teacher wants to check some DVDs out of the library and use them to compile clips for the classroom. Is this lawful? What if the DVDs are copy-protected?

This is one of the more complex copyright situations that school librarians and teachers may encounter, and the answer is different in the K–12 setting than it is for higher education.

First, the easy part. Is it legal to make clip compilations for classroom use? Absolutely. Using short portions of films as a pedagogical tool is a fair use, and fairly common in many subject disciplines.

Our troubles begin when the content is on DVDs or other digital media that is encrypted to prevent unlawful access and copying. In the Digital Millennium Copyright Act (DMCA)

of 1998, Congress prohibited the "circumvention" (breaking) of a "technological protection measure" (encryption, watermarking, password coding) employed by the rights holder to control access to a digital work.[9] The thinking here is that a user who did not pay for access to digital content should not have access. This is quite familiar when one considers that electronic access to newspapers, journals, and other content frequently requires that one purchase a subscription or at least register as a user. To make it difficult to circumvent access controls, section 1201(a)(2) of the Copyright Act prohibits the manufacture of any technology that is primarily used for that purpose.

Oh, but the plot thickens. The law also prohibits the manufacture of technology that is primarily used to break technology employed *to protect the exclusive rights* of the rights holder. This means that if you have lawful access to a work, but want to copy (an exclusive right) a portion of that work for fair use purposes, you cannot do so because the technological tools necessary to circumvent the copy control are illegal and not available to you.

Wrap up:

- Breaking a technological protection measure that controls access is prohibited.
- Creating or making available technology such as a computer program that can break an access code is prohibited.
- Creating or making available technology such as a computer program that can break technologies meant to protect the rights of the rights holder is prohibited.

Congress realized that this arrangement might prove to be problematic for users wanting to make unauthorized but lawful uses of digital content, so it established a triennial "rulemaking" proceeding to check if users either were or were likely to be "adversely affected" by the anticircumvention rules.

A rulemaking is a proceeding that creates regulations—more specific rules to advance, clarify, or set boundaries to broad policies established by Congress. In the DMCA, Congress asked the U.S. Copyright Office to conduct a rulemaking, including a public comment period, to investigate concerns of users who say they have been adversely affected by the anticircumvention provision. The Register of Copyrights is to consider all of the evidence presented, consult with the Assistant Secretary for Communications and Information of the Department of Commerce, and then make a recommendation to the Librarian of Congress, who has the authority to issue the final rule.

The anticircumvention rulemakings have been conducted every three years since 1999. The first rulemakings identified only a few classes of works that were exempt from the DMCA provision. For example, people with print disabilities were allowed to circumvent technology on e-books that prevents the text-to-speech function. In the 2009 rulemaking, seven exemptions were allowed—one that addresses the circumvention of the Content Scrambling System (CSS) on DVDs to allow for the creation of clip compilations. Faculty in all subject disciplines in higher education, college students enrolled in media studies, documentary filmmakers, and private individuals who create noncommercial video compilations for venues like YouTube were allowed to circumvent CSS for the *next* three years.[10] The Copyright Office, after hearing all of the evidence, determined that these users, who require high-quality clips that can only be retrieved by breaking CSS, were adversely affected. The exemption was not extended to K–12 teachers or students in other disciplines because the final recommendation from the Librarian assumed that K–12 educators and any student enrolled in non–media studies type courses did not require high-quality clips. But the rule proves that even the Copyright Office believes that creating clip compilations for classroom, study, and critique are fair uses. While K–12 educators cannot break CSS, they can use other mechanisms—such as screen capture—to create clips.

The exemptions issued by the Librarian of Congress apply only to the act of circumventing the CSS access control, and not to the creation and distribution of a technology that allows this circumvention. Nonetheless, a computer program that can be used to circumvent CSS (DeCSS) is readily available thanks to repeated postings on the Web.

Showing Films Copied from Television or Cable

A teacher may decide to record a TV program on a topic of interest for her class. Can she lawfully show the recorded copy in the classroom? In its entirety? Every year? The *Guidelines for Off-Air Recording of Broadcast Programming for Educational Purposes* is another set of fair use guidelines that addresses these public performances.[11] The guidelines were prepared by representatives from the educational community, rights holders, and creative guilds and unions, and like all guidelines *do not have the force or effect of copyright law.* They were drafted in 1979—before the switch from analog to digital broadcasting, before the dominance of cable television, before the ubiquity of on-demand programming, and before programming could be received and played back on computers—and I find these guidelines particularly quaint. Moreover, the off-air guidelines were written before the landmark 1984 Supreme Court ruling in *Sony Corp. v. Universal City Studios, Inc.,* which determined that "time shifting"—recording broadcast programming to watch at a later time—was a fair use. Are these guidelines even necessary after the *Sony* ruling?

For what it's worth, here are the highlights:

- Nonprofit educational institutions can tape broadcast television for instructional purposes only.
- Only broadcast television programs that are "free of charge" may be recorded off-air. Television programs received by subscription (cable) or for a fee (pay on demand) cannot be recorded.
- A broadcast television program must be recorded simultaneously with the broadcast transmission. The program may only be recorded once, even though the program may air again in reruns or syndication.
- Recordings cannot be made in anticipation of a potential use by a teacher.
- The tape must be screened for class purposes no more than ten days from the date it was recorded. The tape can be screened one additional time for "instruction reinforcement."
- The copy can be retained for forty-five days but then must be destroyed.

The off-air guidelines, like the CONTU guidelines dealing with interlibrary loan, are well established in the library and educational community, leading people to believe that they are unconditional. No taping of cable programming!! No screenings after ten days!! What do you think would happen if you kept the recording for forty-six days??

For educational purposes, one might need to record a cable program, keep the recording more than ten days, and so on. The arbitrary window of ten days is just that—arbitrary. We recognize the problem with the guidelines particularly here—out of date with technology, teaching practices, and our understanding of fair use.

Bear in mind, it is not fair use to record or download programs in order to avoid the purchase of a work that may be readily available in the marketplace. In fact, many television programs are available for purchase or can be licensed and downloaded. Here, the market effect is crucial to the fair use analysis. Recording or downloading programs to create the library's media collection may exceed fair use. But there may be situations where teachers and librarians actually need to hang on to a recording. It may be a one-of-a-kind recording (e.g., of a news event), unavailable for purchase or out of print, and central to course curriculum.

> **Q:** What if a school's curriculum for a particular grade requires the showing of the same taped program year after year?
>
> **A:** Make every effort to locate the recording for sale in the marketplace, then buy it and add it to the library's collection. If it is not available in the market, it may be fair use to perform the tape repeatedly.

Public Performances and Music

Digital natives are accustomed to communicating and making meaning through music, so it is a familiar feature of multimedia student work. The use of music that has been lawfully acquired and stays within the classroom setting is almost always fair, and often transformative. Alas, we must unlearn many of our previous assumptions—that is, if we want to help teachers and students meet their pedagogical and creative goals while acting in accordance with the copyright law. It is (again!) those pesky fair use guidelines that have led us to believe that "up to 10%, but in no event more than 30 seconds, of the music and lyrics from an individual musical work (or in the aggregate of extracts from an individual work), whether the musical work is embodied in copies, or audio or audiovisual works, may be reproduced or otherwise incorporated as a part of a multimedia project."[12]

The multimedia guidelines were prepared in 1996 by representative stakeholders at meetings convened by the Consortium of College and University Media Centers (CCUMC). They have never been endorsed by the ALA but were no doubt helpful to managers of university media centers looking to draw a line in the sand between what's fair and what's not fair. As we have learned, however, there are no "bright lines" regarding fair use. Congress did not intend for fair use to be set in stone, and the courts have frequently reminded us that "freezing" the fair use doctrine, especially in a time of technological innovation, is not prudent.[13]

What about music performed at assemblies, football games, and other venues? (Section 110(1), discussed above, takes care of classroom uses.)

An exception in section 110 comes in handy for noncommercial performances of nondramatic musical works. It excuses many musical performances that typically occur in school, such as orchestral performances, music that accompanies dance performances, the annual

Fair use guidelines had their heyday in the late 1970s and 1980s. The latest attempt to create fair use guidelines—the Conference on Fair Use (CONFU) in the mid-1990s—failed to result in a consensus among the representatives. The meetings were contentious, and since then, guidelines have fallen out of favor. The proposed guidelines that were developed at that time, reprinted in appendix G, are also readily available on the Web.[14]

school concert, and even performances where a fee is charged (under certain conditions below). Section 110(4) allows for the on-site performance of a nondramatic musical work,

> without any purpose of direct or indirect commercial advantage and without payment of any fee or other compensation for the performance to any of its performers, promoters, or organizers, if—
> (A) there is no direct or indirect admission charge; or
> (B) the proceeds, after deducting the reasonable costs of producing the performance, are used exclusively for educational, religious, or charitable purposes and not for private financial gain, except where the copyright owner has served notice of objection to the performance under the following conditions:
> (i) the notice shall be in writing and signed by the copyright owner or such owner's duly authorized agent; and
> (ii) the notice shall be served on the person responsible for the performance at least seven days before the date of the performance, and shall state the reasons for the objection; and
> (iii) the notice shall comply, in form, content, and manner of service, with requirements that the Register of Copyrights shall prescribe by regulation.[15]

But what about performances that are transmitted—for example, when songs are played over the school intercom system during morning announcements and in between class periods? These performances are not excused by this exception but do occur frequently nonetheless. They appear to be "tolerated uses," not of much importance for rights holders. ASCAP and BMI, the primary clearinghouses for music licenses, do not even offer a K–12 license as they do for universities and colleges for music played during football games, during school assemblies, and at graduation.

One important caveat: This exception does not apply to dramatic musical performances. These are performances that include a narrative, such as musicals or operas. I will have more to say about these "grand performing rights" in chapter 7, where I also address recording rights for performances.

What about performances played over the Internet as digital audio recordings? For nonprofit teaching purposes, these performances may be excused by the TEACH Act or fair use. For performances that the library or school might want to post on the open Internet, permission is probably required.

Music Lyrics

Let's say a teacher instructs her students to go to a lyrics website and download and print the lyrics of a song of their choosing. The students are asked to rewrite the lyrics as a song about mathematics and then to perform the song in class. Most of the class performances are longer than thirty seconds and use more than 10 percent of the original song. Doesn't this activity break the copyright law outright?

There are at least two elements in this case that we can deal with in swift fashion. The performance in class is permitted by the section 110(1) exception. And we have learned that the 10 percent and thirty seconds guidelines do not carry legal weight, so we can throw them out altogether. Copying the lyrics and creating a new song may be excused by fair use. Parody, for example, is one of the exemplars of fair use, and it requires that enough of the original work be mimicked in order to make a point. In this case, the resulting parody does not compete in the marketplace for the existing work, so there is no market harm. But even if the resulting work is not strictly parody, it is transformative—it uses the original work in a way not intended by the rights holder and creates something new. Even if the entire work is used (the whole song), that use can be transformative, as we learned in the fair use chapter. And it is not plagiarism, because the students do not claim that they are the authors of the original work.

Lesson plans like this one, where copies are made but the use is fair, are good opportunities to teach students about copyright and plagiarism. Discussions about authorship and building on the ideas of others, especially as a way of learning, might be a good place to start. You could remind your students that with school assignments there's more latitude because educational fair uses are favored. Fair use of these songs may not extend to the commercial arena, and posting the parodies online—outside the sanctity of the nonprofit educational classroom—may negatively affect the fair use assessment.

Incidental Public Displays and Performances

Especially with the advent of smartphones and tablets, a person can easily and inadvertently make a public performance. On the subway, a fellow rider might see the movie you are watching on your iPad. A nearby pedestrian might hear a ringtone when someone calls you. Or your neighbor may hear you playing the radio (loudly) while you're washing your car. These uses are "de minimis"—so trifling and temporary that they do not rise to the infringement level. You should not concern yourself with them.

Public Displays

The exclusive right of copyright related to public display—the right to show a copy of a work or an image of a work—has not drawn the kind of attention that the public performance right has. Not, that is, until the digital age. I've never been asked if the glass exhibit case in the library that displays book covers is an infringement, but I am asked about the digital copies of book covers displayed on the library's website. Of course, the situations are different because with digital displays, whether public or not, a copy is made. We tend to believe that the problem is the *copy*, even though Congress held a different assumption when it was drafting the Copyright Act of 1976, where the public display right was first codified.

The public display right is granted for "literary, musical, dramatic, and choreographic works, pantomimes, and pictorial, graphic, or sculptural works, including the individual images of a motion picture or other audiovisual work."[16] Phonorecords are excluded from the list because they can only be performed.

Displays occur with original works—such as original pieces of art—but more frequently with copies of works, such as that reproduction of a Salvador Dali that hangs outside your office door. Displays also occur when you use equipment to project an image on a screen or when you view an image on a computer.

Many public displays, however, are excused by section 109, our favorite "first sale" exception. Subsection (c) grants the owner of a lawfully acquired copy the right to display that copy at the place where the copy is located, even though this display might be public. If you buy a photograph or painting to hang on the library walls, you do not have to contact the rights holder for prior permission even though many people will eventually see the poster because the library is a public place. Note, however, that this exception does not extend to displays of works that are transmitted on television or by computer networks. Confused? Me, too.

In the 1960s, when Congress began work on the copyright revision legislation that eventually became the Copyright Act of 1976, the concept of public display included

> not only . . . displays that occur initially in a public place, but also acts that transmit or otherwise communicate a . . . display of the work to the public by means of any device or process. The definition of "transmit" . . . is broad enough to include all conceivable forms and combinations of wired or wireless communications media, including but by no means limited to radio and television broadcasting as we know them. Each and every method by which the images . . . comprising a . . . display are picked up and conveyed is a "transmission," and if the transmission reaches the public in [any] form, the case comes within the scope of [the public display right].[17]

What about scanning and posting the images of book covers on the library website, then? Is this an infringement of the public display right *and* the reproduction right because a copy is made? Yes, but it's fair use.

Purpose of the use: Libraries use book cover images for nonprofit purposes, often accompanied by a book synopsis or review to promote reading or to highlight new library acquisitions, which leans in favor of fair use.

Nature of the work: Book covers can be highly original works of art, which leans against a finding of fair use.

Amount of the work used: Generally the entire book cover is used, but often in thumbnail form, which is less than optimum for making additional copies of the book cover. This could go either way.

Effect on the market for the work: The book cover image is not a substitute for the actual book that has been purchased by the library. Similarly, there isn't a market for the display of book cover art that would be harmed by the display. This factor also weighs in favor of fair use.

PowerPoint Presentation of a Book

Let's say the superintendent has been invited to your school to read a storybook to the entire school assembly. So the students can read along with her, she plans on scanning the book's pages and making it into a PowerPoint presentation that will be projected on a big screen at the back of the auditorium. Changing the format and copying the entire book? Wouldn't this be wrong?[18]

First, a copy of the book will be created without the authorization of the copyright holder. Then, during the school assembly, both the rights of public performance (reading aloud to a group) and display (showing images and text from a book to a group) will also be implicated. There is no specific exemption that excuses this apparent infringement—other than fair use. But there are other issues that we can clarify.

1. Changing the format of the book is not an infringement per se (sometimes changing the format of a work is perfectly fine), but it is making another copy of the work. Librarians and educators need to unlearn the rule that "changing the format" is an automatic infringement.
2. The fact that more than 10 percent of the work has been copied is irrelevant because the amount of a work that is copied is only one factor of the fair use assessment and is not determinative. Percentages are arbitrary figures that almost never appear in the copyright law.

The beauty of the fair use exception is that it can be applied to any use of a copyright-protected work in any case at any time. The situation at hand is the issue.

Analysis:

Purpose of the use: This use is nonprofit, and it supports the socially beneficial use of reading. This factor favors fair use.

Nature of the material being used: The work is likely fictional, and it includes creative visual elements that are deserving of thicker copyright protection, so this factor leans against a fair use reading.

Amount of the work being used: The entire work is being used, which leans against a fair use ruling—though one could argue that for a story to be effective it must be read in its entirety. Let's call the amount factor insignificant in this case.

Effect on the market for the work: Will sales for the work be displaced by this event? No: it is unreasonable to believe that because of the reading, the rights holder will lose sales. But what about license fees? The existence of or potential existence of a royalty market for the use is not determinative. The fourth factor is not more important than the others, and the existence of a royalty market does not mean that a use is unfair. The effect on the market is only one factor under consideration, and it must be assessed along with the other factors. In any event, there really is no market for the reading of books at school assemblies.

Determination: Fair use.

Some alert readers may be thinking this use could be more reasonable if a document camera were used to project the images on the screen, eliminating the need to make an entire copy of the work. This is true. Often there are ways to adjust behavior to make uses more acceptable. On the other hand, in this instance, the difference probably is not significant enough to justify the added complication of using a document camera. Remember, fair use is a rule of reason.

Murals

In general, painting murals of book covers or book characters on the walls of the library or the school to promote learning and for noncommercial purposes is a fair use. However, there is always an element of risk—some rights holders who want to maintain greater control over their works may choose to bring an infringement suit. This was the case when Disney asked three Florida day-care centers to remove images of Goofy, Donald Duck, Mickey Mouse, and Minnie Mouse that they had painted on the exterior of their buildings. The day-care centers, lacking the resources for a fight in court, agreed to remove the characters.[19]

Some rights holders turn to other laws, such as trademark, to control how their distinctive company slogans, symbols, or characters are used. Particularly because of trademark law, protected images on school building exteriors should probably be avoided—especially if they involve great cost. On the other hand—and there always is another hand with copyright law—if the mural is truly a transformative use of the characters, the risk is diminished. For example, if the mural shows a child with a whirlwind of thoughts above his head, and those thoughts include a variety of characters from cartoons and films, the fair use argument becomes very strong.

Once the mural is done, who holds the copyright? The muralist or the school?

The answer in the first instance depends on whether the muralist is a school employee who prepared the mural within the scope of her employment. If the muralist was not a school employee, then the copyright belongs to the muralist, unless the contract between the school and muralist included an assignment of the copyright to the school. When schools and libraries hire independent contractors to create works—murals, photographs, software, promotional materials, and so forth—they must take great care to make sure that the independent contractor has assigned or otherwise licensed her copyright to the institution. Otherwise, when the institution wants to make a new use of the work in the future, it may find itself paying again for something it already purchased. (The exception to the general rule of the independent contractor owning the copyright occurs when the work is specially commissioned as a contribution to a collective work, as an instructional text, as a test, or as an answer material for a test. But even this exception applies only if the parties agree in writing that the exception applies. So the school should always have a written agreement with independent contractors that specifically addresses the copyright ownership issue.)

Images Found on the Web

Because copyright notice and registration are no longer required under the copyright law, you must assume that everything you find on the Web—including photographs and other images, graphics, and text—is protected by copyright. Initially, many people thought, "Hey, these things must be free for the taking, otherwise they wouldn't be up on the Web." More recently, rights holders of materials on websites have been using more prominent copyright statements, Creative Commons license notices, or other ownership alerts. You should always take the time to read these notices, even when using images or other materials from "free" websites. "Free" means different things to different people. For example, "royalty free" may mean that you do not have to pay the photographer or artist but you still have to pay a fee. Terms of use contracts may restrict the way you can use the image. Sometimes website owners have no right to claim that the images posted have been cleared for rights. This language is typical:

> [Name of company] does not represent or make any warranties that it owns or
> licenses any of the mentioned, nor does it grant them. It's your sole responsibility
> to make sure that you have all the necessary rights, consents and licenses for the
> use of the image.[20]

In such cases, treat the images as if they are protected by copyright and, if you want to use an image for educational purposes, conduct a fair use analysis.

SUMMARY

In this chapter, we examined the exclusive rights of public display and performance and discussed exceptions to those rights that are available to nonprofit educational institutions, including libraries. The most important things to know:

- Public performance licenses are never required for classroom screenings (unless there is an explicit license restriction).
- Your rights of fair use are not affected by the existence of specific exceptions and limitations for public performance and display. In other words, you can always use the fair use exception—whether other exceptions apply or not.
- Most of the real-life activities in schools and libraries that have a copyright element are not covered in the law, so you must rely on fair use.
- Licenses, in general, trump copyright law.

NOTES

1. Marc Prensky, "Digital Natives, Digital Immigrants," *On the Horizon* 9, no. 5 (October 2001). Author's copy available at www.marcprensky.com/writing/Prensky%20-%20Digital%20Natives,%20Digital%20Immigrants%20-%20Part1.pdf.
2. 17 U.S.C. § 101.
3. Id.
4. *CleanFlicks of Colorado, LLC, v. Soderbergh et al.*, 433 F. Supp. 2d 1236 (D. Colo. 2006).
5. Pub. L. No. 1099, 119 Stat. 218, 223–24.
6. 17 U.S.C. § 110(2)(A), (B).
7. See 17 U.S.C. § 110(2)(C), (D).
8. See 17 U.S.C. § 110(2), (2)(D)(i).
9. Circumvention is not a copyright infringement because it does not violate any of a rights holder's exclusive rights.
10. Exemption to Prohibition on Circumvention of Copyright Protection Systems for Access Control Technologies, 75 *Federal Register* 43825 (July 27, 2010).
11. *Guidelines for Off-Air Recording of Broadcast Programming for Educational Purposes*, H.R. Rep. No. 97-495, at 8–9 (1979). (See appendix D.)
12. "Fair Use Guidelines for Educational Multimedia" (see appendix G).
13. H.R. Rep. No. 94-1476, at 66 (1976).
14. See www.ccumc.org/assets/documents/MMFUGuidelines.pdf and Bruce A. Lehman, *Final Report to the Commissioner on the Conclusion of the Conference on Fair Use*, November 1998, U.S. Patent and Trademark Office, www.uspto.gov/web/offices/dcom/olia/confu/confurep.pdf.
15. 17 U.S.C. § 110(4).
16. 17 U.S.C. § 106(5).
17. H.R. Rep. No. 94-1476, at 63 (1976).
18. This is a paraphrased version of a question posted on LM_NET.
19. "Cartoon Figures Run Afoul of Law," *Chicago Tribune*, April 27, 1989, 26.
20. This language appears in the "Terms of Use" agreement for ImageFree.com at www.imagefree.com/Home/TermsOfUse, last updated January 26, 2010.

CHAPTER 6
Veronda and Lena Want to Digitize Textbooks

In this chapter, we will review a number of copyright situations that crop up when teaching, creating lesson plans, using class websites, and drawing on materials found on the Web. Every day in the process of teaching, educators make uses that implicate the exclusive rights of copyright—reproduction, distribution, derivative works, and public performances and display. Works or portions of works are copied throughout the school day. In the digital environment, even more copies are made—such as the copies stored temporarily in a computer's RAM.

Why is this not a copyright problem? Congress understands that teaching and learning will involve the use of protected works in a variety of ways, and in all formats, including digital. We know that the constitutional purpose of the copyright law is to advance learning. To ensure that the economic rights of rights holders do not expand to the point of being an obstruction to learning and innovation, Congress provides several exceptions to schools, libraries, archives, and other cultural institutions. Exclusive rights—the rights to market and sell copyright-protected materials—do not dominate the copyright equation. Imagine if every use of a protected work required prior authorization. We would never have the time or money to do the job of teaching.[1] We would have to kill library storytime because after all, that's an unauthorized public performance.

In addition to specific exceptions designed particularly for educators and librarians, we also have fair use. While not all uses of protected works in the nonprofit educational setting will be fair, the majority are. It's just a fact. In addition, in the educational setting, we often use works in transformative ways, favored by the courts as being fair uses.

Given the copyright leeway librarians, educators, and students have, when *is* a use an infringement? Because we almost always want to use works for nonprofit educational purposes (fair use factor one), it may be useful to highlight the remaining factors of fair use— nature of the publication, amount used, and effect on the market for the work—to tease out uses that are problematic or at least open to discussion. Sometimes a questionable use can be tailored back and made more clearly lawful.

NATURE OF THE WORK USED

You'll remember that the second factor of fair use has to do with the kind of work you want to use. Factor two can be significant because such a wide variety of resources are used for teaching—textbooks, anthologies, licensed databases, primary resources, and open content with fewer copyright restrictions on use. Textbooks still dominate in some subject areas and when standardized tests are linked to a defined curriculum. But online content that accompanies textbooks may have its own terms of use.

Unpublished works have a thicker copyright layer than published works, and fictional, creative works have more protection than factual materials. From this vantage point, asserting fair use with respect to an unpublished work or a fictional work is more challenging. For example, copying a fictional story from the *New Yorker* for student use tilts further from fair use than copying an article out of *Newsweek*. Copying a graph instead of a graphic is generally fair. Copying a local news program weighs more toward fair use than copying a motion picture. As the Supreme Court ruled, "The second statutory factor . . . calls for recognition that some works are closer to the core of intended copyright protection than others, with the consequence that fair use is more difficult to establish when the former works are copied."[2]

> The public domain is not just a place where old things go to die. It is something that exists also within protected works. Textbooks are filled with facts that have no protection. Even within more creative works, pieces of the public domain exist.

AMOUNT OF THE WORK USED

We know that fair use guidelines that specify the percentages of works that can be used have limited value, but of course, under factor three, using more of a work is more of a problem than using less of a work. Be mindful of instances where you want to copy an entire work. Is it really necessary? Use other methods when you can—for example, place portions of materials on reserve rather than making entire copies for each student.

EFFECT ON THE MARKET

Factor four asks us to consider the market for the work. Out-of-print works may still be protected by copyright, but copying these works has little if any effect on the market. Consumables—workbooks, sheet music, practice tests—are meant to be purchased for each student. Copying these—assuming they are currently being sold—has a direct impact on the market for the work. Occasionally, resources intended for teachers are labeled with notices that state that copies can be made for each student.

Textbooks: Aren't They Sacred?

Q: Our school district has not yet received its order of textbooks for the semester. Can we copy the one textbook that we have and make copies for the students?

A: Because the textbooks have been purchased, it is reasonable to make copies until the order arrives, but it is probably sufficient to copy only the portion necessary in the immediate future—a chapter or two. Another option is to post the first chapter on a password-protected course website and remove it once the students' textbooks arrive. And any hard copies should be collected and destroyed once the textbooks arrive.

Q: One of our teachers wants to use a textbook that is out of print. I called the publisher, who does not have any copies of the old edition in stock, and they have no plans to reprint it. They are promoting a new edition instead. I searched BookFinder, Alibris, and Amazon but could only locate two used copies. I don't think it is right to make copies of an entire textbook.

A: The fair use argument is bolstered by the fact that you have made a good faith effort to purchase additional copies that are just not available, and there is no negative effect on the market for the old edition. However, making copies of the old edition arguably harms the market for the new edition, which likely includes material from the old edition. So copying the old edition technically harms the market for the old material included in the new edition. This is a situation that might be solved by thinking creatively. Because you want to help the teacher meet his teaching goals, look for other ways his need can be met without copying an entire textbook. Can the teacher identify distinct portions of the book that he finds most valuable—ideally, any sections that are no longer included in the new edition—and copy those rather than the entire book? Could individual chapters of the book be posted on a password-protected website and then removed when no longer needed for instruction? Can the two or three available copies be placed on library reserve and still meet the educational needs of the students?

Textbooks: Aren't They Sacred?

Q: Some students have five or six heavy textbooks that they have to carry around all day. If we have purchased print copies for each student, can we make digital copies that the students can keep on their laptops or e-readers?

A: Instead of digitizing and loading entire textbooks onto the students' computers or mobile devices, it may make more sense to put additional copies of the textbooks in the classroom or in the library for short-term reserve loan. If there is a real need to make digital copies, could portions be placed on a password-protected website?

Q: Our math teacher uses a textbook that is now out of print. We try to buy additional copies at the beginning of every year and keep them all in our depository. When school starts, each student checks out a textbook, but the teacher usually has to make several photocopies of the first two chapters to accommodate extra students until after the add/drop date.

A: Here, every effort has been made to buy additional copies of the out-of-print textbook. The limited amount of copying that takes place before finalization of enrollment is fair use.

Q: The English department purchased new textbooks this year. In the teacher's version of the textbook, a CD was included that has all of the short stories that appear in the textbook. The teachers would like to make a copy of the CD for each student. Is this a copyright problem?

A: First, check if there is a license agreement associated with the CD. The contract terms may address this issue, likely indicating that the CD is provided for archival purposes and not for further reproduction and distribution. If there is no license agreement, consider the four factors of fair use. Because the students already have the short stories in their textbooks, it seems overkill to make additional copies of a CD that could be easily copied. Unless there is some transformative use that requires ready access to digital copies, the use is not fair.

MULTIPLE COPIES FOR CLASSROOM USE

As we have seen, Congress makes a specific exception for multiple copies for classroom use in section 107 of the Copyright Act, stating that

> the fair use of a copyrighted work, including such use by reproduction in copies
> or phonorecords or by any other means specified by that section, for purposes
> such as criticism, comment, news reporting, teaching (*including multiple copies
> for classroom use*), scholarship, or research, is not an infringement of copyright.

Okay, but if you make copies of a magazine or newspaper article for an entire class, aren't you taking money that authors could be collecting in royalties?

Perhaps, but the fourth factor of fair use (market effect) is not the sole determining factor. If a use is fair, it means that the use can be made without prior authorization from the rights holder and without paying a royalty fee.[3] Still, some believe that if a rights holder has established a method to be paid for every use, then the rights holder must always be paid. If this were true, it would mean that all fair uses—even quoting from a work—would be unfair.[4] Law professor Lydia Pallas Loren puts it this way:

> This is circular reasoning at its best.... The ability to prove economic injury merely by
> showing that one has established a system to charge for a certain kind of use portends
> that a smart copyright owner will always prevail on the fourth fair use factor.... The
> argument that "lost" permission fees are proof of fourth factor harm has as its premise
> the legal conclusion at issue: that the use at issue is not a fair use and, therefore, the
> owner is allowed to charge permission fees for such use. If a copyright owner labeled
> his permission system "the department for charging fees for criticism, comment, news
> reporting, teaching (including multiple copies for classroom use), scholarship and
> research," then the attempt to control fair use would be more obvious. Consideration
> of the permission fees allegedly "lost" in determining whether a use is a fair use is
> inappropriate because no fees are required unless the use is not a fair use.[5]

Yet, in the important *Betamax* fair use case, the Supreme Court suggested that "to negate fair use one need only show that if the challenged use should become widespread, it would adversely affect the *potential* market for the copyrighted work."[6] Meanwhile, another court rejected the notion that fair use decisions should be based on lost permission fees, arguing that "it is wrong to measure the detriment to plaintiff by loss of presumed royalty income—a standard which necessarily assumes that plaintiff had a right to issue licenses. That would be true, of course, only if it were first decided that the defendant's practices did not constitute 'fair use.'"[7]

What do you do with conflicting opinions? Go back to the fair use factors and consider other options.

- Is the use transformative?
- Is the material copied from a book purchased by the school or to a journal to which the library has a continuing subscription?

- If not, can the library buy the original work?
- Is the material primarily factual in nature? Or is it more fictional, like a short story?
- Can you put the materials in a library database and give students a link rather than make copies?
- Can the teaching objective be met in another way?
- Can one copy be made available to the students through library reserve, so students could make their own individual copies under the conditions of section 108 (library reproductions)?

Ultimately, you will need to make a decision based on your own thoughtful analysis of the situation. Your decision will likely be affected by the amount of risk your institution is willing to take, but recognize that the likelihood that this use will lead to legal action is small.

CURRICULUM MATERIALS GO DIGITAL

Publishers have good reason to move to an all-digital textbook market—after initial development and start-up, production costs are lower, updating content is easier, and retention or resale of the textbooks can be reduced. The resale market for textbooks is fairly strong, and publishers naturally want to curtail it. Used copies of textbooks that have not been reissued or updated enjoy second and third lives in the hands of new students without the publisher being compensated. In the digital environment, we have become fairly accustomed to renting access to information rather than purchasing to own copies. Licensing terms can be enforced through technology—any copying could be tracked, and (best of all, at least

> **Q:** A high school art student comes into the library in search of photos and other images to use in a collage project. She prints from the Internet and photocopies from magazine articles and books. Is this okay? What should be the proper instruction from the school librarian?
>
> **A:** The art collage is the quintessential example of a transformative use—using elements of other works to create something new, with new meaning, and in ways not intended by the original creators. The school librarian should explain that even if the works included in the collage are protected by copyright, they can be used without prior authorization in ways that are considered fair. Asking that the students provide a full citation for each work used helps to reinforce the notion of authorship. Of course, if the collage contains small parts of a large number of images, providing attribution may be impractical.

for the rights holders) access to the content can be turned off at the end of the school year. One student, one textbook, one year, the end.

Using Materials Found on the Web

We have learned that creative works found on the Web have the same copyright protection as their analog counterparts. This is true even for "born digital" works that have no analog counterpart. But sometimes in the frenzy of pulling materials together for class instruction, we forget that the exclusive rights of copyright are implicated. Some still have the notion that if it's on the Internet, it must be free. Copyright exceptions—library reproductions, first sale, and the like—don't necessarily translate to digital resources. The TEACH Act is the only amendment to the 1976 analog copyright law that addresses teaching and the digital environment—and it doesn't do a good job of it. There is danger in regulating digital knowledge and creativity any further, because technology continues to move at a rapid pace. By making new laws that fail to keep up with this pace, Congress demonstrates a lack of solid understanding of how teaching has changed and how students learn. Worse, by holding teaching hostage to prerequisites and checklists—as we have seen with TEACH—it adds to the confusion and stifles pedagogical choices.

Making Audio Copies

Librarians and teachers may want to make an audio recording of a book for students who have print or learning disabilities or are learning English as a second language. When existing copies of the audiobook are not available in the marketplace, this is a clear fair use. (Under certain circumstances, this audio recording may also fall within a specific exception for reproduction for the blind and print disabled, 17 U.S.C. § 121, also known as the Chafee amendment, discussed below in more detail.)

Can you post the audiotape on a protected course website? Or make an MP3 file to load on an iPod for the student? When a copy is made to address a specific user need because there is no other option available, keeping that copy "secure"—accessible only by the student who needs the work—supports the fair use analysis. Adding the recording to the collection or lending the recording to others who do not have a similar need changes the argument of fair use.

Let's say a teacher wants to change the format of a book on tape in order to have a digital file to use online for distance learning or for other reasons. In general, just as with videotapes, one should not transfer titles wholesale to newer formats even if there is no digital copy available in the marketplace. But there may be instances when a digital file is absolutely necessary to meet the teaching goal, and even the TEACH Act allows for these instances. You would be crossing the line, however, if the transfer from analog to digital were done "just in case" someone might need it. The teaching need must be real and restricted to teaching of that class. On the other hand, as discussed above in chapter 3, fair use might allow a format change for preservation purposes.

What if you have a lawfully acquired digital copy of an audio recording—say an MP3 file—that includes technological protection measures (TPMs) that prevent you from copying or loading the file to the protected course website? Can you circumvent the TPMs in order to make the necessary copy? Under the Digital Millennium Copyright Act, the answer is no. However, if you can locate an analog copy of the audio recording, you can digitize that copy to meet the teaching need.[8]

Creating Teaching or Access Tools

Educators may create their own lesson plans or worksheets based on textbooks or other protected resources that have been assigned to the students. For example, a math teacher might create a supplementary worksheet drawing on math examples from the textbook. An educator may create an index to accompany a short story anthology. A fair use analysis can help determine if the use is fair, but first keep in mind the limitations of copyright protection. Math examples, in particular formulas and equations, may not be protected by copyright at all because they are facts. Likewise, a list of words that provides locators indicating where the words occur within the protected work—an index—may not meet the requirements of copyright protection.

SUPPLEMENTAL CLASS RESOURCES

Educators often want to augment learning by providing supplemental resources that are not included in traditional textbooks. Sometimes it is a spur-of-the-moment idea to dupli-

cate an article from the newspaper or tape a relevant program airing on a cable network. Most of these instances are fair, but is it all right to plan ahead and then copy, distribute, or otherwise use protected resources without getting permission? It depends. The preamble to the fair use section of the copyright law provides "multiple copies for classroom use" as an example of fair use. On the other hand, the reproduction exception for libraries in section 108(g) states that copying and distributing works under the section 108 exceptions should be restricted to "isolated and unrelated reproduction or distribution of a single copy or phonorecord of the same material on separate occasions"—indicating that Congress frowns on organized and regular copying. And on the other hand (your third), section 108 also says that nothing in that section affects the right of fair use provided by section 107. Great, now what?

Course Packs

In the college or university setting, supplemental packets of works are called course packs, which students typically have to purchase.[9] Most of the purchase price pays for permissions to make the reproductions, typically acquired through the Copyright Clearance Center (CCC), a nonprofit company that collects fees on behalf of rights holders. It stands to reason that schools should be paying these same fees when educators compile course packs. Interestingly, though, CCC focuses its service on colleges and universities or business institutions. Perhaps K–12 schools have financial resources that are so limited that CCC does not even bother to establish a K–12 service.

One way to assess whether one should pay a permission fee for creating a K–12 course pack is to look at each protected work individually, making the fair use assessment. Permission may be necessary when educators want to copy a large portion of a work or a work that is creative in nature. This would rule out the need to ask permission for short articles in newspapers, factual works, or works in the public domain.

Music in the Classroom

Playing music in the classroom—such as background music played during art class or music played during dance class—are public performances excused by section 110(1), which allows

Q: A music teacher would like to copy the song "Hey Jude" onto thirty CDs to use with his music students. Is this legal?

A: First, a fair use evaluation:

Purpose—nonprofit, educational (fair)
Nature of the publication—highly creative (not fair)
Amount—the entire song (not fair)
Effect on the market for the work—(not fair in that copies of the song, if required as a resource for the class, could be purchased, one copy for each student through a download service like iTunes)

A librarian could tease out information from the teacher—why are thirty individual copies necessary to meet the teaching goal? Perhaps the song could be played during class—eliminating the need to make the copies. Could a copy of the song be made available in library reserve for the students? How about posting the song on the password-protected course website that only the students can access?

Q: Our digital video class wants to make their own music videos to accompany popular songs. They will use the entire song in the video. Must the students ask for copyright permission, and if so, whom do we ask? What if they want to enter the video into a student contest or festival?

A: If the performances of the video are restricted to the classroom or to a secure course website, the use is fair. Once outside of the classroom, permission may be necessary from a music-licensing company like BMI, ASCAP, or SESAC. On the other hand, literally millions of such videos are found on YouTube, suggesting the rights holders have grown tolerant of such uses.

Q: Our school purchases all of our band music for each instrument and for each student. So if there is music for the oboe, we would buy a copy for each student who plays the oboe. But because students lose their music, the band director has taken to filing the original, purchased pieces and making a copy for each student. This way, if the tuba player loses his piece, the entire band doesn't suffer. The copies are not kept. Each year we buy new copies.

A: Even though this is straightforward copying of an entire musical score that is creative in nature, because the school has purchased the entire set for each instrument and student, the effect on the market is minor. However, if the instrument-specific scores can be purchased separately, consider purchasing an additional copy each time one is lost. In the meantime, the original copy can be used.

Q: What is considered fair use of song lyrics? I'm a Spanish teacher and it is helpful to do translation activities with song lyrics familiar to the students. I find song lyrics online, make copies for the students, and use the lyrics to create learning activities.

A: This appears to be a fair use in that the song lyrics are used in conjunction with nonprofit education and in a transformative way. The recording industries, however, argue that song lyric websites are capitalizing on the work of musical artists, usually by selling advertisements, without compensation. So is it okay to use lyrics that are posted to websites that may be infringing? Because the courts have not ruled definitively that these uses are infringing, thus far it is just the opinion of the recording industry that they are infringing. You may be able to refer to the terms of use on the lyrics website. It may state that the website has indeed licensed the use of the lyrics that appear on the site. But just because the website owner has worked with the rights holders to lawfully post the lyrics, you can't assume that you can use the lyrics in the classroom. Those pesky terms of use may also state that third parties can use the lyrics only for "personal, noncommercial use." Another user right lost in a world of nonnegotiable licenses!

nonprofit educational institutions to play music, including entire songs, in the face-to-face classroom without authorization. Other uses of musical works—inserting portions into a PowerPoint presentation, doing a cover version of a musical work, or copying music onto new formats—usually require a fair use analysis, as you can see from the examples above.

AND NOW THE BIG MUDDLE

While most of the materials found on the Internet are protected by copyright, your use of them *may* be governed by a nonnegotiated license agreement associated with the content. When you click on the "Yes" button to access the content, the terms of the license detail how you can use the content. Of course, most of us do not read the license terms—they are written in legalese, tiny print, why bother! There is no clear consensus by the courts that nonnegotiated licenses are legally binding, and at least part of the lack of clarity has to do with varying interpretations of "preemption"—whether a license (a state law) can take away a right you have under the federal copyright law. Another complication is the theory that some nonnegotiated licenses are more binding than others. Contracts where the user must actively assent to the license terms by clicking on the "Yes" icon (a click-through or click-wrap license) are probably more binding than a license printed on shrink-wrap packaging (a shrink-wrap license) or one that appears at the bottom of a web page in tiny letters (a browse-wrap license). In any case, the courts are more likely to enforce these contractual terms against an institutional user than an individual user, on the theory that the institution is more legally sophisticated than an individual consumer.

Music Downloads

When downloading music from a lawful website, one must agree to the license terms before using the service. Many of these terms limit the use of the downloaded music to "personal use." Here is an example of the terms of use for MediaNet, a company that sells digital music files.

> 8. Usage Rules and Restrictions
> Upon payment of the Permanent Download Fee MediaNet grants You a non-exclusive, non-transferable right to use the Permanent Download in accordance with the following usage rules ("Usage Rules") and subject to the provisions of these Terms of Sale and the Terms of Use:
>
> a. Your use of any Permanent Downloads purchased via the MediaNet Service is conditional upon Your prior acceptance of these Terms of Sale and the Terms of Use, including, without limitation, the Usage Rules set out therein.
>
> b. You shall be entitled to export, burn or copy Permanent Downloads solely for *Your personal, non-commercial and entertainment use and not for any redistribution.*
>
> c. Any burning or exporting capabilities shall not constitute a grant or waiver of any rights of the copyright owners in the Content or any related content provided as part of the MediaNet Service.
>
> d. Permanent Downloads can only be downloaded once per transaction. You may copy, store, transfer or burn a single Permanent Download to a CD an unlimited number of times provided that such use is solely for Your own personal, entertainment and non-commercial use. *Once you have burned a Permanent Download to a CD, you agree not to copy, distribute, or transfer the track from that CD to any other media or device.*

e.   Unless otherwise expressly authorised in these Terms of Sale, *any reproduction, redistribution, transmission, sale, broadcast, public performance, sharing, rental or lending, adaptation, sub-license, modification, promotion, commercial use, sale, transfer, assignment or other use of the Permanent Downloads provided through the MediaNet Service, including, without limitation, any use that requires a synchronization license with respect to the underlying musical composition, is a violation of copyright law* and expressly prohibited without the prior written consent of the Content Owner.

f.   Permanent Downloads may not be used as a musical "ringer" in connection with phone calls.

g.   You understand that once You have purchased and received a Permanent Download it is Your sole responsibility not to lose, damage or otherwise destroy the Permanent Download and MediaNet shall have no liability to You for any such loss, damage or destruction.[10] (italics added)

Can we just ignore these licenses when we know that we are using the content in lawful ways? This is a decision that you have to make. The risk is low, but "contracts of adhesion" have been accepted by some courts as binding even though they bypass rights you have under the copyright law. Librarians should continue to tell their vendors and other companies that they need to supply a different set of terms for educational institutions and libraries. The situation will only grow worse as more content is available only in digital formats, as we already see with music.

User Generated Content (UGC)

The saying that the Internet allows anyone to be a publisher is certainly true. The Internet is replete with user generated content—discussion lists, Wikipedia, YouTube, blogs, Facebook, Goodreads, and websites like "Men Who Look Like Kenny Rogers." All of this content is protected by copyright as soon as it is created and posted online. When users contribute their content to these sites, there is frequently a license agreement lurking in the background that describes how the website owners plan to use that content.

> **Q:** Some of our teachers are interested in saving educational YouTube clips to another medium for classroom use in order to get around our school filters, which prevent them from screening directly from the site. What should we be concerned about, since YouTube owns the content?
>
> **A:** First, remember that YouTube posts terms of use that restrict use of the site to personal, noncommercial use. This is not a yes or no click-wrap license but the browse-wrap variety, which carries less legal weight. Second, YouTube does not own the content but has a nonexclusive right to publish and use the content on its site." The original creator of the video—who makes the decision on how her rights of copyright are licensed—is still the rights holder.
>
> I suggest to librarians that, ultimately, they should make a decision by conducting a fair use analysis even though YouTube "lives" in a licensed context rather than a federal copyright law context. If your use is not fair, then contact the original creator of the video and ask for permission, because YouTube is not the rights holder.

SERVING STUDENTS WITH DISABILITIES OR SPECIAL LEARNING NEEDS

Congress and the courts have recognized that making accessible copies in various formats for students with disabilities is fair use. When drafting the Copyright Act of 1976, House members offered this guidance about fair use:

> Another special instance illustrating the application of the fair use doctrine pertains to the making of copies or phonorecords of works in the special forms needed for the use of blind persons. These special forms, such as copies in Braille and phonorecords of oral readings (talking books), are not usually made by the publishers for commercial distribution. . . . While the making of multiple copies

or phonorecords of a work for general circulation requires the permission of the copyright owner, a problem addressed in section 710 of the bill, the making of a single copy or phonorecord by an individual as a free service for blind persons would properly be considered a fair use under section 107.[12]

This is a significant statement because Congress provides no qualifications or prerequisites for making accessible copies. In the U.S. Supreme Court case of *Sony v. Universal City Studios*, the court stated: "Making a copy of a copyrighted work for the convenience of a blind person is expressly identified by the House Committee Report as an example of fair use, with no suggestion that anything more than a purpose to entertain or to inform need motivate the copying."[13]

School librarians and educators should feel confident when making a copy of a work for a student with print disabilities, especially when the accessible format is unavailable in the marketplace. This would include making a large-print copy of a class resource, making an audio file of a print publication, and using machine readers that require digital copies. Whether this broad statement about the application of fair use, without any preconditions, applies to making accessible copies for people with hearing disabilities, learning disabilities, or physical disabilities is not explicitly stated, but you can feel confident that fair use would apply. One reason we can feel confident is the fact mentioned above in the House report: accessible copies are often not available in the marketplace, and copyright exceptions try to address such "market failure." Another instance of market failure is when the rights holder takes too long to respond positively for permission to make the accessible use.

Section 121, aka "The Chafee Amendment"

Does it get better? Sort of, but not really. In 1996, Congress added what is commonly known as the Chafee amendment to the Legislative Branch Appropriations Act of 1997 providing a specific exception for nonprofits serving people with print disabilities.[14] This amendment was based on previous agreements between the National Library Service and the Association of American Publishers.[15] Apparently, the National Library Service, in operation since 1931, sought permission from rights holders whenever they produced accessible copies of lawfully acquired books even after the 1976 act, because they believed that prior permission was always necessary and that the use was not fair. But as we learned from the TEACH Act and section 108, exceptions that address specific activities (public performances via digital technologies, library reproduction for purposes of preservation and replacement, making digital copies) tend to take on the quality of an audit or checklist, requiring certain things to be true before the exceptions are allowed. While the Chafee amendment was welcome news to those who had previously spent the time to clear permissions, if they had relied on fair use instead, users with print disabilities could have been more effectively served. Furthermore, when nonprofit agencies serving the print disabled always ask for permission, they set up a pattern of behavior that indicates that the use is not fair, establishing an expectation that rights will always be sought. Can fair use and the Chafee amendment live side by side in harmony? Certainly. But when a specific amendment is passed, people mistakenly come to believe that the amendment defines all that is possible under any notion of fair use.

Chafee Amendment Prerequisites

Section 121 allows nonprofit organizations or governmental agencies (including schools and libraries) with a *primary* mission to serve the blind or others with print disabilities the right to make an accessible copy of a published nondramatic literary work and distribute that copy to a user without authorization. The statute refers to "*a* primary mission," not "*the* primary mission." So it is unclear whether the exception applies to public, school, or academic libraries that serve a general population as well as people with print disabilities.

Section 121 is also limited in that accessible copies must be in specialized formats made exclusively for the blind or print disabled. This limitation has been met by the National Library Service through the use of a specially designed playback machine for books on tape (in addition to copies made in Braille). The idea, of course, is to ensure that only a person with a visual disability would need to use such equipment. Additional equipment for reading with the playback machine such as amplifiers for people with hearing disabilities can be requested, but an application certified by a recognized authority is required. Readers who do not have electricity can get a solar-powered battery for their playback machine, but this, too, requires an additional application form.[16] Making accessible copies of publisher-produced worksheets and tests is not allowed, yet these are the very materials students with disabilities need at their disposal in a timely fashion.[17]

A further confusion is that although the statute refers to the "blind or other persons with disabilities," that phrase has been defined in essence as the blind and the print disabled:

> The following persons are eligible for service:
> 1. Blind persons whose visual acuity, as determined by competent authority, is 20/200 or less in the better eye with correcting lenses, or whose widest diameter of visual field subtends an angular distance no greater than 20 degrees.
> 2. Other physically handicapped persons are eligible as follows:
>   a. Persons whose visual disability, with correction and regardless of optical measurement, is certified by competent authority as preventing the reading of standard printed material.
>   b. Persons certified by competent authority as unable to read or unable to use standard printed material as a result of physical limitations.
>   c. Persons certified by competent authority as having a reading disability resulting from organic dysfunction and of sufficient severity to prevent their reading printed material in a normal manner.[18]

As one can see, section 121 has many preconditions that must be met to ensure that only the qualified user with disabilities has access to reading materials and specialized equipment. Under fair use, anyone (not just specialized agencies) could create an accessible copy (in any format) of any type of work (not just published nondramatic literary works) for a person with any disability (with or without proof of disability).

To complicate matters (because life *should* be hard), there are a number of other federal and state laws that define access to information for the disabled in various ways. The

Q: We have a machine that scans books and then reads the text to our special needs students. Can the teacher save the scanned book to use later with another student? Can more than one student use the scanned information if we have only one copy of the book?

A: The Chafee amendment does not mention whether accessible copies can be retained, but this is clearly a fair use when the accessible copies are used only for students with disabilities in a nonprofit educational setting and only at the point of need. Remember that the accessible copies are not available to purchase, so there is no market harm.

Q: We have many students who require books on tape for their Individualized Education Program (IEP). While I do my best to secure copies of the books, many people feel it's okay to make copies of the books because it is legally required that the students have these books available.

A: Making an entire copy of a book to meet the needs of persons with disabilities is also a fair use. The fact that students require these tapes for their IEP and these requirements are state law does not override copyright law, but it is a compelling element of the fair use equation. Factor one: this is a nonprofit educational use for students with special needs. Factor two: the nature of the work is a published audiotape, a title that is required as part of the IEP. Using another work instead is not an option because of the IEP. Factor three: the amount used will be the entire tape, which can generally be a problem, but in order to meet the teaching goal, students need to have access to the entire work. Factor four: the effect on the market is nil as long as the titles required are not readily available for sale in audio form.

As long as you have done a diligent search to locate the audiotapes for purchase, go ahead and make the tape. If the same books are required next year, I would search again for the tapes in the market because they may have become available. I would also label each tape with a copyright warning statement like "Further reproduction or distribution of this work may be a violation of copyright" for good measure. There are times when the audiotape is available for purchase but would not be effective as a teaching tool. For example, students with reading disabilities or students learning English as a second language may need a book to be read to them in a particular fashion, perhaps slowly or emphasizing particular words. When this is the case, the fair use justification remains reasonable.

IDEA Act helps state libraries provide accessible copies to K–12 students with disabilities but limits collection efforts to the provision of textbooks only.[19] State boards of education often develop their own policies on making information accessible for all students, leading one to wonder if it is better to follow the law (which may be restrictive) or the policies of state boards (which may be less restrictive).

KEY LEARNINGS

- Many educational uses of protected content are fair, particularly when they are transformative. Some uses that go beyond fair use can be tailored in ways that make the use likely fair. Tailoring might involve restricting access to the copy, providing the copy by another means such as library reserves, or copying only the portion necessary to meet the teaching goal.

- Required texts and consumables like workbooks should be purchased for each student unless there are extenuating circumstances (the item is unavailable for purchase and out of print).

- Fair use factor four—effect on the market—is only *one* of the fair use factors you must consider when making your decisions. And the existence of a mechanism to collect royalty payments does not automatically make a use unfair.

- Content on the Web, including user generated content, is protected by copyright unless you know otherwise (the creator has forfeited all exclusive rights and the work is in the public domain).

- There are often licenses associated with content found on the Internet that can sidestep copyright exceptions. Courts have not agreed whether these licenses are legally binding, but click-wrap licenses—where a user must actively assent to a license before gaining access to the protected works—are more likely to be legally binding than agreements that do not require consent.

- Copying works in an accessible or alternative format for students with disabilities is often fair use because of market failure.

- Specific limitations to copyright, such as those in section 121 of the Copyright Act, are often more restrictive than fair use.

NOTES

1. Law professor John Tehranian has described how an average professor could rack up $12.5 million in liability damages if rights holders pursued every infringement made in the professor's typical day—such as forwarding e-mail messages or inadvertently reproducing artworks displayed in public places when taking a photograph of birthday festivities at a restaurant—revealing the dichotomy between copyright law and behavioral norms. Tehranian, "Infringement Nation: Copyright Reform and the Law/Norm Gap," *Utah Law Review* 2007 (2007): 543–48, http://ssrn .com/abstract=1029151.

2. *Campbell v. Acuff-Rose Music, Inc.*, 510 U.S. 569, 586 (1994).

3. *Campbell*, 510 U.S. at 585 n.18 (1994): "If the use is otherwise fair, then no permission need be sought or granted."

4. The Associated Press has partnered with iCopyright to charge licensing fees for quotes as short as five words. See Mike Masnick, "iCopyright Sues AP . . . ," *TechDirt*, December 7, 2010, www.techdirt .com/articles/20101206/00125012141/icopyright-sues-ap-saying-it-didnt-promote-pay-up-to -quote-5-words-service.shtml.

5. Lydia Pallas Loren, "Redefining the Market Failure Approach to Fair Use in an Era of Copyright Permission Systems," *Journal of Intellectual Property Law* 5, no. 1 (Fall 1997).

6. *Sony Corp. of America v. Universal City Studios, Inc.*, 464 U.S. 417, 451 (1984).

7. *Williams & Wilkins Co. v. United States*, 487 F.2d 1345, 1357 (1973).

8. 17 U.S.C. § 112(f)(2).

9. *Princeton University Press v. Michigan Document Services, Inc.*, 99 F.3d 1381 (6th Cir. 1996). The practice of paying license fees for course packs in higher education grew out of a few cases in the 1990s where courts found commercial photocopy centers liable for infringement for photocopying course packs. In those cases, the courts rejected the photocopy centers' argument that the photocopying constituted a fair use. However, those cases involved copying by commercial firms, not by the universities, faculty, or students. Conceivably, the result may have been different if the copying had been done by a noncommercial actor. Moreover, fair use jurisprudence has evolved over the past twenty years. Those cases might have been decided differently now.

10. MediaNet, "Terms of Sale for Permanent Downloads," www.mndigital.com/legal/terms-of-sale .html, agreement as of September 30, 2010.

11. YouTube, "Terms of Service," www.youtube.com/t/terms.

12. H.R. Rep. No. 94-1476, 94th Cong., 2d Sess. (1976).

13. *Sony*, 464 U.S. at 456.

14. Title 17, § 121.

15. *Congressional Record*, July 29, 1996, page S9066.

16. National Library Service, "Playback Machines and Accessories Provided on Free Loan to Eligible Individuals and Institutions," *NLS Factsheets*, January 2009, www.loc.gov/nls/reference/factsheets/ playback.html.

17. Title 17, § 121(b)(2).

18. National Library Service, "Eligibility of Blind and Other Physically Handicapped Persons for Loan of Library Materials," www.loc.gov/nls/eligible.html.

19. Individuals with Disabilities Education Act (IDEA), 20 U.S.C. § 1400.

CHAPTER 7
The School Has a Talent Show

High school just would not be complete without extracurricular activities. They help students build social skills and good work habits, teach them how to work in teams, and involve them in the community—in addition to providing fodder for college applications. Unfortunately, extracurricular activities come with their own set of copyright implications. What happens to the fair use analysis when the use of a copyright-protected work is no longer educational? Who "owns" the extracurricular programs? What if parents want to videotape the school play? Do you need public performance rights for every musical work played at the school concert? What if tickets will be sold to raise funds? And now the drama teacher wants to post last year's musical revue on the school website!

I am tired already.

As we have learned, copyright law rarely addresses these questions specifically, so fair use—the all-purpose user exception—often guides our way. With no definitive answers, we must make do with common sense and an understanding of the four factors. Take some comfort in the fact that in the larger scheme of things, rights holders are unlikely to sue schools for copyright infringement. They have bigger fish to fry and more lucrative companies to sue.

LET'S PUT ON A SHOW!

For those who remember older Hollywood movies, the dialogue goes something like this:

> *YOUNG MAN:* I know. Let's put on a show!
>
> *YOUNG WOMAN:* That's a great idea. You can sing.
>
> *YOUNG MAN:* And you can dance.
>
> *SECOND YOUNG WOMAN:* And we've got all of those old costumes in the attic upstairs!!

Alas, reality is not an old Mickey Rooney–Judy Garland classic. Anyone who has ever organized a program, planned a public event, or staged a performance knows that a whole lot of work—especially behind the scenes—is involved. When the big day comes, you pray that all of the pieces will fall into place. And of course, you have to think about copyright.

Live Performances

There is an exception in the copyright law that allows for unauthorized live performances of protected works, addressing many school public performances, including those typical of a student talent show. This exception is section 110(4), which exempts

> performance of a nondramatic literary or musical work otherwise than in a transmission to the public, without any purpose of direct or indirect commercial advantage and without payment of any fee or other compensation for the performance to any of its performers, promoters, or organizers, if—
>
> (A) there is no direct or indirect admission charge; or
>
> (B) the proceeds, after deducting the reasonable costs of producing the performance, are used exclusively for educational, religious, or charitable purposes and not for private financial gain, except where the copyright owner has served notice of objection to the performance under the following conditions:
>
>   (i) the notice shall be in writing and signed by the copyright owner or such owner's duly authorized agent; and
>
>   (ii) the notice shall be served on the person responsible for the performance at least seven days before the date of the performance, and shall state the reasons for the objection; and
>
>   (iii) the notice shall comply, in form, content, and manner of service, with requirements that the Register of Copyrights shall prescribe by regulation.[1]

Plain language: Public performances of protected works are allowed without prior authorization from the rights holder as long as

- the performance is live and not transmitted to the public in any other way;
- the work used is a song or written work that is not a play or a screenplay; and
- no performers, organizers, or promoters are paid.

If you charge an admission fee, the proceeds must be used for educational, religious, or charitable purposes only. If you do plan to charge an admission fee, the rights holder can stop the performance if he sends a notice to the school seven days prior to the scheduled performance. (Pretty unlikely, but you never know.)

What is covered by this exception:

- reading poetry or a passage from a novel aloud
- singing a song
- performing orchestral music
- dancing original steps to musical accompaniment
- playing a song in the background of a live performance
- twirling a baton, juggling, performing magic tricks, performing feats of strength (and so on) with music playing in the background

Dramatic Literary or Musical Works

The 110(4) exception does not apply to musicals, operas, plays, screenplays, pantomimes, choreography, and other dramatic works. Why? As with motion pictures, the economic value of these works depends almost entirely on the performance.

To collect on that value and to ease your ability to pay for a license, various permissions systems have been established to collect royalties for these rights. If a school wants

Q: A theater arts teacher uses movie scripts for student productions. The shows are performed during the school day for an audience of schoolchildren and no admission is charged.

A: Section 110 does not address this question specifically, but fair use does. The performances are used to teach acting and other theatrical skills in the nonprofit educational environment—this is fair.

Q: Our school plans to stage *West Side Story* this spring. What copyright permissions will be necessary? What other rules should concern us?

A: The school must obtain "grand performing rights" from the rights holder. Sometimes plays or musicals are "restricted"—not allowed at all—so be prepared with a second choice. After the rights for the performance are obtained, purchase scripts for each actor and anyone else (e.g., stage crew) who might require one. The script will generally contain additional information regarding the performance itself or publicity.

Q: The school's mixed choir wants to sell DVD copies of its annual school performance. Are permissions necessary?

A: Yes. A mechanical license can be obtained through the Harry Fox Agency.

Q: At the talent show, three students plan to stage a scene from *Death of a Salesman*. Is permission necessary?

A: This is arguably a fair use since only one scene will be performed.

Performing Derivative Works

Students may wish to perform their own version of a story, perhaps turning it into a play or readers' theater. They might want to change the lyrics of a popular song or do a parody of a cable program. Within the school environment, these uses are fair. Students should cite the original work to recognize the author and alleviate plagiarism concerns.

to perform a dramatic work that includes music, dancing, dialogue, staging, and so on, "grand performing rights" must be sought directly from the rights holder in most cases. Even if a student wants to perform just a scene or portion of a musical, section 110(4) does not apply unless the performance excludes any dramatic elements (staging, costumes, dancing, and so on). In other words, singing "Everything's Up to Date in Kansas City" from *Oklahoma!* without any dialogue and costuming is likely excused by section 110(4).

It is easiest to contact a musical or theatrical licensing house to begin the permissions process.[2] If you do not know the rights holder, they can provide that information. Some of these licensing houses also sell scripts with license conditions that further restrict what you can do with the play or musical. Typical licenses do not allow variations in the script or changes in character names or locales, or may restrict advertising and require that men play male roles and women play female roles.

Recording Performances

No doubt, a parent or teacher will want to record all or part of the talent show, orchestral performance, or play, embarrassing the children who are in the production. Section 110(4) is an exception to the public performance right, not the reproduction right, so it does not permit this recording. As a practical matter, recording the performance is not a serious copyright problem because the copies get minor exposure outside of the family or classroom. But once that copy gets outside of the school or is publicly available on the school

Q: One of the students running for class president is using Clinton's presidential campaign theme "Don't Stop Believing." Is this a copyright problem?

A: No, short phrases cannot be protected by copyright, although they may be protected by trademark law. This should not be a concern unless the use of the phrase actually confuses potential consumers for the product associated with the phrase—in this case, a song by Journey.

website, concerns rise to some extent. There is increased likelihood that the rights holder may learn of the copy and perhaps seek a licensing fee or ask for swift removal of the copy. Based on your risk-aversion level, you may wish to acquire "mechanical rights" for musical performances. A mechanical license can be obtained from the Harry Fox Agency. This license allows the recording of a cover version of another song and is required by statute for commercial recordings. A synchronization license allows for the recording of a scene set to music, as in a music video. In the nonprofit educational setting, even outside of the classroom, these licenses probably are not necessary (because of fair use), but they should be considered if the plan is to sell the recordings.

OTHER EXTRACURRICULAR ACTIVITIES

The School Dance

School dances usually have titles or themes like *Some Enchanted Evening*, *Stairway to Heaven* (an oldie but a goodie), *A Midsummer Night's Dream* (really old) to give the event

some personality. These titles can be used without concern because titles have no copyright protection.

A license to spin records at the dance or play music in the background at school educational events or for cheerleading is not required for K–12 schools but may be necessary for competitions. Contact ASCAP, BMI, or SESAC and ask for a "special event" license.

Student Clubs

The French club wants to watch French films. The debate team wants to make photocopies of current news stories as fodder for

Tip: "Stairway to Heaven" is hard to dance to. It's too long, and then it has that fast section.

their extemporaneous debates. The chess club photocopied a list of strategies from *How to Reassess Your Chess: The Complete Chess-Mastery Course*. The gaming club is holding another tournament as a fund-raiser.

Many of these uses are in the trivial category, but you still may have concerns, wondering what those kids are up to. One idea is to distribute a flier with a few pointers on copyright law. You may feel it is necessary to set limits on what students can do in their clubs so everyone is following the same set of rules. It is true that club activities are not 100 percent

Yearbook

Q: I am the yearbook advisor and want to be in compliance with the copyright law. Can we use three lines of the song "Unforgettable" in the school yearbook? The yearbook does not make any profit.

A: This is a fair use query. Let's consider the four factors of fair use. Under factor one, we look to the purpose of the use. This use is part of extracurricular but nonprofit activities. This places us in the middle of the factor one scale. The second factor asks what kind of material we are using. Here we are using a popular song, already published and produced by many others, but creative in nature. This places us somewhere in the middle of the factor two continuum. Third factor: how much of the work is used? Just three lines, which leans toward a fair use reading on factor three. Finally, is the use affecting the market for the work? Not in the least. You will discover that fair use determinations will end up being a mix of fair and unfair and a mix of importance and insignificance. Even with the trifling use of three lines of a song, we have areas—like the creativity of the work in factor two—that can cause people to doubt their fair use analysis. This use, however, is a typical example of fair use—quoting from a work. My suggestion is that this use is not only fair but trivial in nature.

Q: Our principal wants to give each student a CD copy of the year's performances—everything from the talent show to the student chorale. Is there a copyright problem? Most of the songs are protected by copyright.

A: Reproduction of music covers requires a mechanical license from the Harry Fox Agency. But also take an extra step and place a copyright warning statement on each CD to remind people that further reproduction or distribution, particularly online, may be an infringement of copyright. I would also include a notice "not for resale" or "for nonprofit purposes only."

Q: The student council has created a slide show with over two hundred images, most of them photographs of the students. They want to play this slide show, which includes background music, at our last student assembly. They have timed the slides to match up with certain songs. Now they want to sell DVD copies for five dollars. I'm not comfortable with this.

A: Many schools ask parents to sign releases for their children that allow them to participate in clubs or have their photos taken. This greatly reduces any problems with photographs of the students. The public display of the slides at assembly, even with background music, does not present a problem. This is a onetime, nonprofit event that is also transformative in nature because the photos and music are used to create a new work with a new meaning. Selling copies is not problematic because of the minimal effect on the market for the work. In other words, it is very unlikely that a consumer would choose to purchase your school's DVD instead of purchasing the songs themselves. The wider distribution of the DVDs seems more serious, because additional copies will be made and may be further reproduced. Labeling the DVDs with a "not for resale" and copyright warning statements demonstrates that the school recognizes that further reproduction and distribution may rise to an infringing use. Of course, a warning label does not prevent all further unauthorized uses, but it does help and shows good faith. All of the songs used should be cited somewhere in the production.

educational (as understood in the copyright law), and they may stray into commercial territory if the club is trying to raise money, so the first factor of fair use may straddle the continuum.

Student Broadcasts

Many schools have studios or other production facilities that students use to produce their own morning newscasts for the school. Copyright concerns may arise when students incorporate other works in their program.

The transmission of music over a closed-circuit video system at a school is a public performance because the performance occurs at a place that is open to the public and more than a few friends or family members hear the music. As we have learned, the right of public performance is an exclusive right of the copyright holder, and exercising a right of copyright without prior authorization is an infringement. Some public performances are excused under section 110(1), however, such as the right to perform music in the course of "face-to-

A Word about Gaming

Digital games are often sold to the consumer with a terms of use license, the click-through agreement that you must assent to for the game to operate. These licenses are designed for individual, noncommercial use and often restrict group activity like public performances. Many libraries sponsor gaming tournaments that may involve public performances or public displays. Libraries might also use gaming tournaments as fund-raising events, which might be viewed as violating the terms of use agreement if fund-raising is considered a commercial activity. Nonetheless, rights holders have not raised any concerns with these contract violations.

face" classroom teaching. The argument could be made that section 110(1) does apply given the situation—for example, if the newscast was produced by the communications class and viewed on monitors by students in separate classrooms. Another option is fair use. I think this is fair for the following reasons: although not educational, it is noncommercial; small portions of songs are played; students are likely to be exposed to different music, which is socially beneficial and could lead to future sales; and, assuming the music was lawfully purchased, the juxtaposition of student art with the music could be considered a transformative use—often ruled fair.

Another way to approach this situation is to rule that the performance is trivial and so minor (de minimis) that there is no need to worry about it.

Q: Our high school distributes a student-produced morning newscast within our building via cable. May we show clips from current motion pictures in conjunction with student-produced reviews during the program?

A: This is another public performance and, again, there is no definitive answer or specific area of the law that addresses this question. The use of the clips is not for true curriculum purposes, so classroom exemptions might not apply. One could argue that because the use is nonprofit, and only short clips of works are used, and because there is no negative effect on the market (assuming the motion picture videos were lawfully obtained), this activity is fair. In addition, section 107 of the copyright law specifically mentions criticism and comment as an exemplar of fair use, strengthening the fair use argument. The fair use case is also bolstered by the fact that only those within the school building have access to the morning newscast. I tend to view this activity as fair, but you must make the call.

WHO OWNS THE COPYRIGHT TO STUDENT WORKS?

In general, the students own the copyright, but student works often are included in school publications with a copyright statement indicating that the school holds the copyright. As we know, creative works often have more than one rights holder. If the school's arrangement or recording of the students' work reaches the modicum of creativity required (e.g., the school records ten selected students reciting poems they wrote), the school may hold rights to the larger work. Students who are very interested in protecting their copyright may want to label the original works with their name and a copyright symbol. When a long feature article written by a student for the school newspaper includes a copyright notice, the student has visibly asserted copyright. This may be helpful to students seeking to use the work in the future for a portfolio. The student photographer may wish to do the same when her photos appear in school publications. Students often create works in clubs or groups as well, which could raise issues of joint authorship. Teacher supervisors may wish to discuss copyright with the students involved to clarify any misunderstandings before they arise.

SCHOOL COPYRIGHT POLICY

With so many uses of copyrighted works in both the educational and extracurricular settings, it is impossible to monitor what everyone is doing. Don't even try. A good solution is to have a copyright policy—not necessarily to list every copyright and copywrong, but to communicate your school's copyright philosophy. Such a policy should focus on the mission of your school—to advance learning through teaching. The policy should acknowledge that schools and libraries have special status under the copyright law and that copyright is less restrictive for them than for commercial users. The policy should also include a statement about the importance of copyright law to education—the school community is both a creator of new content and a user of existing content. The policy I am describing here is more of a vision statement—how the copyright law is key to the educational mission.

Longer, more detailed policies are often developed. These policies typically address the more procedural issues—who can use the photocopiers, when do you have to ask for permission, who should be consulted if you are unsure about your use of a protected work. A procedural policy is one that emphasizes how the school community is expected to behave in regard to the copyright law. Too often, the procedural policy has less to do with copyright law and more to do with what the school believes will keep it out of legal trouble. If everyone follows the policy, a standard of behavior is soon established. One problem with such policies is their shortsightedness—spelling out how one should behave now does not address the many ways that teaching will evolve, particularly in regard to the use of new technology. Such a policy becomes out of date quickly. Worse, these policies, when very restrictive, can negatively affect teaching and learning by trying to control actions that may or may not be infringing. The spontaneous, serendipitous bursts of creativity in teaching and in learning can be quelled for fear of breaking the law.

A third type of copyright policy is a copyright education guide—a sort of Copyright 101. This policy explains what copyright is, the requirements for copyright protection, the exclusive

rights of copyright, fair use, and so on. Copyright 101 sets out to inform the educational community about the law and may, instead of including directives, make the assumption that once people are informed, they are smart enough or can be trusted enough to make their own decisions about copyright. Copyright 101 is handy to have and can be the basis of in-service copyright training. Supplementing the educational materials with illustrative case studies will bring the ideas home to teachers and students.

Ideally, the school copyright policy should be a combination of the three styles—informative, but with enough leeway in interpretation to allow for unforeseen uses of protected works in teaching and learning. The Web offers a wealth of copyright policies for schools. Select a few and ask the school community for feedback. If the community has the opportunity to help develop the copyright policy, it will more likely accept it and follow it.

Is There a Special Copyright Law for Disney?

I was once asked this question. There is only one U.S. copyright law, and it applies to everyone. Disney has a reputation for enforcing its copyrights with extraordinary rigor. It wants to control its copyrights, but of bigger concern is control over how the original work is used. Derogatory or satirical versions of popular characters—like Mickey Mouse—may cast a bad light on the wholesome and family-friendly Disney we have all come to know and love. Some of these uses may be fair, but Disney threatens legal action and people usually back down. What may be equally problematic is that Disney, in these instances, suppresses free speech.

KEY LEARNINGS

- Live, noncommercial performances of nondramatic literary and musical works do not require prior copyright permission.
- Public performances of dramatic literary and musical works often require prior permission from the rights holders, unless they qualify as a fair use. Musical and theatrical licensing houses have been established to assist with the royalty process.
- Recordings of performances that include copyrighted material may require a license from the Harry Fox Agency.
- Developing a school copyright policy should be a shared activity within the school community, from assessing need, identifying content, and determining the various ways the content is conveyed.

NOTES

1. See 37 C.F.R. 201.13, "Notices of objection to certain noncommercial performances of nondramatic literary or musical works."
2. Dramatic Publishing, Samuel French, Baker's Plays, and Pioneer Drama are examples of play and music publishing houses. Some megarights holders like Rodgers and Hammerstein have their own theatrical licensing divisions that are readily accessible on the Web.

CONCLUSION
Gary LeDuc Says Good-bye

Copyright exists to advance learning by encouraging the dissemination of creative works. The public policy objective of the law can be easily overlooked when all we want to do is understand enough of the law to be able to answer our day-to-day copyright concerns. But the copyright law does not have a Q&A section. There are no easy and definitive answers. And even if the law included a cheat sheet, copyright cannot be considered in isolation. Other things must be taken into account—specific court decisions as well as any identifiable trends, the mission and objectives of the school, and the degree of risk, to name just a few. These additional circumstances are not set in stone, nor are they necessarily consistent with one another. It is a mixed bag with changing parts. Copyright is a gray area.

As more information is available in digital form, copyright seems—in a way—"old school." Licensing determines what we can do with digital works, and unlike copyright law, nonnegotiated contract terms are all too clear. Take it or leave it, no exceptions. Copyright exceptions like library lending may not be an option under a license agreement. But copyright, unlike licensing, remains important because it advances a policy that benefits the public, those people whose interests we represent. Public policies should reflect how we want the world to be, and the values of librarians and educators—who believe in information access, learning, and intellectual freedom—are all reflected in the copyright law.

So copyright has its muddles, its occasional futility, its contradictions, but it is based on a very good thing—getting information to the people.

GRAY IS BETTER THAN BLACK AND WHITE

Admittedly, it can be annoying to not know the right answer when dealing with a copyright issue. In this book, I have tried to emphasize that you will be most successful with copyright when you engage in critical thinking instead of resorting to a cheat sheet. Knowing the theoretical construct of copyright law—the reason *why* we have copyright law in the first place—builds a way of thinking. The four factors of fair use—section 107 of the law—are the criteria used to make good judgments. Our commitment to professional values commands that librarians and educators take a leadership role in dealing with copyright law at our institutions. Have the courage to *see* the gray area, and the opportunities to advance the mission of libraries and education will be your reward.

APPENDIX A
SLMS and Copyright:
A Survey

Q1. You have been a working school library media specialist for

ANSWER OPTIONS	RESPONSE PERCENTAGE	RESPONSE COUNT
0–2 years	12.0	34
2–5 years	15.1	43
5–10 years	22.5	64
over 10 years	50.4	143

	answered question	284
	skipped question	0

Q2. Do you consider your knowledge of copyright to be

ANSWER OPTIONS	RESPONSE PERCENTAGE	RESPONSE COUNT
Excellent	9.2	26
Good	79.9	227
Not so good	10.9	31

	answered question	284
	skipped question	0

Q3. Do you consider yourself the point person at your school for copyright questions?

ANSWER OPTIONS	RESPONSE PERCENTAGE	RESPONSE COUNT
Yes	86.6	246
No	13.4	38

	answered question	284
	skipped question	0

Q4. Is your role as copyright point person acknowledged in your school?

ANSWER OPTIONS	RESPONSE PERCENTAGE	RESPONSE COUNT
Yes	54.9	156
No	45.1	128

	answered question	284
	skipped question	0

Q5. Do you provide copyright training for school administrators, teachers, and/or students? (check all that apply)

ANSWER OPTIONS	RESPONSE PERCENTAGE	RESPONSE COUNT
Administrators	27.1	77
Teachers	50.0	142
Students	64.4	183
I do not provide training.	29.2	83

	answered question	284
	skipped question	0

Q6. How confident do you feel responding to copyright questions and issues at your school?

ANSWER OPTIONS	RESPONSE PERCENTAGE	RESPONSE COUNT
Not confident at all.	4.2	12
Some questions still stump me.	36.3	103
Fairly confident, I know the basics.	53.5	152
Very confident.	6.0	17

	answered question	284
	skipped question	0

Q7. The purpose of the copyright law is to make sure that authors and creators are fairly compensated for their work.

ANSWER OPTIONS	RESPONSE PERCENTAGE	RESPONSE COUNT
True	82.7	234
False	17.3	49

	answered question	283
	skipped question	1

Q8. Do you feel you have had adequate training to deal with the kinds of copyright issues that come up at school?

ANSWER OPTIONS	RESPONSE PERCENTAGE	RESPONSE COUNT
Yes	40.6	115
No	41.3	117
I'm not sure I know what training I need.	18.0	51

	answered question	283
	skipped question	1

Q9. Are copyright education workshops required at your school?

ANSWER OPTIONS	RESPONSE PERCENTAGE	RESPONSE COUNT
Yes	9.5	27
No	90.5	256

	Comments	18
	answered question	283
	skipped question	1

Q10. As far as you know, do the majority of teachers and administrators follow the training provided to them?

ANSWER OPTIONS	RESPONSE PERCENTAGE	RESPONSE COUNT
None of the time	3.7	10
Some of the time	54.8	148
Most of the time	18.1	49
Don't know	23.3	63

	answered question	270
	skipped question	14

Q11. The purpose of the copyright law is to give authors and creators property rights over intangible creations.

ANSWER OPTIONS	RESPONSE PERCENTAGE	RESPONSE COUNT
True	56.4	154
False	43.6	119

	answered question	273
	skipped question	11

Q12. Does your school follow copyright guidelines like the "Guidelines for Classroom Copying in Not-for-Profit Educational Institutions with Respect to Books and Periodicals" that provide a guide for the percentage of a work that can be lawfully copied?

ANSWER OPTIONS	RESPONSE PERCENTAGE	RESPONSE COUNT
Yes	47.9	135
No	34.0	96
I have no idea what you are talking about.	18.1	51

answered question 282
skipped question 2

Q13. If there was one thing you wanted to know/learn about copyright today, it would be

	RESPONSE PERCENTAGE	RESPONSE COUNT
	58.1	165

answered question 165
skipped question 119

Q14. The following issues are the most difficult to explain to schoolteachers and administrators (check all that apply):

ANSWER OPTIONS	RESPONSE PERCENTAGE	RESPONSE COUNT
Public performance of videos or DVDs	65.5	184
Scanning materials (when is it lawful and when does it go over the line?)	40.9	115
Faculty or students making multiple copies of protected works	59.4	167
Fair use	50.5	142
Plagiarism	17.8	50
Using protected works for extracurricular activities (school concert, PTA meeting, student play, etc.)	56.2	158
Public domain (when is a work in the public domain?)	26.0	73

ANSWER OPTIONS	RESPONSE PERCENTAGE	RESPONSE COUNT
Posting protected materials on the school website	33.1	93
Student projects that involve the use/ mixing of protected works (background music, images found on the Web, student-produced videos)	63.7	179
Using iPods to download music	22.1	62
When to follow a license and when to follow copyright law	33.8	95
When you can make a backup copy	34.2	96
When to seek permission	37.7	106
How to seek permission	45.2	127
Teachers using course software like Blackboard, what are the copyright rules?	25.6	72

comments	21
answered question	281
skipped question	3

Q15. In general, do you think that students and teachers tend to infringe copyright without realizing it?

ANSWER OPTIONS	RESPONSE PERCENTAGE	RESPONSE COUNT
Yes	92.9	261
No	7.1	20

answered question	281
skipped question	3

Q16. In general, do you think students and teachers are well aware that they are violating the law, but they just go ahead and do it anyway?

ANSWER OPTIONS	RESPONSE PERCENTAGE	RESPONSE COUNT
Yes	47.7	134
No	52.3	147

answered question	281
skipped question	3

Q17. The purpose of the copyright law is to encourage the creation and distribution of works to benefit the public.

ANSWER OPTIONS	RESPONSE PERCENTAGE	RESPONSE COUNT
True	43.5	118
False	56.5	153

answered question	271
skipped question	13

Q18. If you knew a classroom teacher was infringing copyright, what would you do?

ANSWER OPTIONS	RESPONSE PERCENTAGE	RESPONSE COUNT
Ignore it.	5.3	15
Ignore it at first.	7.4	21
Approach the teacher and try to explain why the actions are illegal.	83.4	236
Report the incident to the principal.	3.9	11
Call the police or other authorities to report the incident.	0.0	0

answered question	283
skipped question	1

Q19. If your school has a copyright policy, who wrote it?

	RESPONSE PERCENTAGE	RESPONSE COUNT
	44.4	126

answered question	126
skipped question	158

Q20. If the copyright policy is accessible online, please provide the web address.

	RESPONSE PERCENTAGE	RESPONSE COUNT
	14.4	41

answered question	41
skipped question	243

Q21. A teacher wants to read a poem at the graduation assembly and also wishes to include the poem in the graduation program with proper attribution. Is this a copyright infringement?

ANSWER OPTIONS	RESPONSE PERCENTAGE	RESPONSE COUNT
Yes, it is infringing.	30.8	86
No, it is lawful.	37.3	104
I don't know.	31.9	89

	answered question	279
	skipped question	5

Q22. Do you believe that other schools have been sued or taken to court because they have infringed copyright?

ANSWER OPTIONS	RESPONSE PERCENTAGE	RESPONSE COUNT
Yes	89.2	247
No	10.8	30

	answered question	277
	skipped question	7

Q23. Do you know that schools have been sued for copyright? Explain.

	RESPONSE PERCENTAGE	RESPONSE COUNT
	35.2	100

	answered question	100
	skipped question	184

Q24. Which statement best describes you?

ANSWER OPTIONS	RESPONSE PERCENTAGE	RESPONSE COUNT
I choose to be strict about complying with copyright to protect the school from litigation.	37.6	103
To be honest, my approach to copyright is wishy-washy—sometimes I am strict about compliance and other times I let it slide.	39.4	108
My approach to copyright is lenient because I believe many school activities where protected materials are used are lawful.	23.0	63

	answered question	274
	skipped question	10

Q25. Should the school library media specialist be an advocate for fair use? Why or why not?

	RESPONSE PERCENTAGE	RESPONSE COUNT
	71.8	204

answered question	204
skipped question	80

Q26. Have you ever written your congressional representative or senator expressing a view on copyright legislation?

ANSWER OPTIONS	RESPONSE PERCENTAGE	RESPONSE COUNT
Yes	6.4	18
No	93.6	263

answered question	281
skipped question	3

Q27. If you are interested in participating in a short phone interview about copyright and your school, please provide your e-mail address below. Interview information that may be included in the book will remain anonymous.

	RESPONSE PERCENTAGE	RESPONSE COUNT
	19.4	55

answered question	55
skipped question	229

Author survey sent to subscribers of the LM_NET discussion list in May 2008.

APPENDIX B

Agreement on Guidelines for Classroom Copying in Not-for-Profit Educational Institutions with Respect to Books and Periodicals

The purpose of the following guidelines is to state the minimum and not the maximum standards of educational fair use under Section 107 of H.R. 2223. The parties agree that the conditions determining the extent of permissible copying for educational purposes may change in the future; that certain types of copying permitted under these guidelines may not be permissible in the future; and conversely that in the future other types of copying not permitted under these guidelines may be permissible under revised guidelines.

Moreover, the following statement of guidelines is not intended to limit the types of copying permitted under the standards of fair use under judicial decision and which are stated in Section 107 of the Copyright Revision Bill. There may be instances in which copying which does not fall within the guidelines stated below may nonetheless be permitted under the criteria of fair use.

GUIDELINES

I. **Single Copying for Teachers.** A single copy may be made of any of the following by or for a teacher at his or her individual request for his or her scholarly research or use in teaching or preparation to teach a class:
    A. A chapter from a book
    B. An article from a periodical or newspaper
    C. A short story, short essay or short poem, whether or not from a collective work
    D. A chart, graph, diagram, drawing, cartoon or picture from a book, periodical, or newspaper

II. **Multiple Copies for Classroom Use.** Multiple copies (not to exceed in any event more than one copy per pupil in a course) may be made by or for the teacher giving the course for classroom use or discussion; provided that:
    A. The copying meets the tests of brevity and spontaneity as defined below and,
    B. Meets the cumulative effect test as defined below and,
    C. Each copy includes a notice of copyright

Definitions

Brevity

(i) **Poetry.** (a) A complete poem if less than 250 words and if printed on not more than two pages or, (b) from a longer poem, an excerpt of not more than 250 words.

(ii) **Prose.** (a) Either a complete article, story or essay of less than 2,500 words, or (b) an excerpt from any prose work of not more than 1,000 words or 10% of the work, whichever is less, but in any event a minimum of 500 words.

(Each of the numerical limits stated in "i" and "ii" above may be expanded to permit the completion of an unfinished line of a poem or of an unfinished prose paragraph.)

(iii) **Illustration.** One chart, graph, diagram, drawing, cartoon or picture per book or per periodical issue.

(iv) **"Special" works.** Certain works in poetry, prose or in "poetic prose" which often combine language with illustrations and which are intended sometimes for children and at other times for a more general audience fall short of 2,500 words in their entirety. Paragraph "ii" above notwithstanding such "special works" may not be reproduced in their entirety; however, an excerpt comprising not more than two of the published pages of such special work and containing not more than 10% of the words found in the text thereof, may be reproduced.

Spontaneity

(i) The copying is at the instance and inspiration of the individual teacher, and

(ii) The inspiration and decision to use the work and the moment of its use for maximum teaching effectiveness are so close in time that it would be unreasonable to expect a timely reply to a request for permission.

Cumulative Effect

(i) The copying of the material is for only one course in the school in which the copies are made.

(ii) Not more than one short poem, article, story, essay or two excerpts may be copied from the same author, nor more than three from the same collective work or periodical volume during one class term.

(iii) There shall not be more than nine instances of such multiple copying for one course during one class term.

(The limitations stated in "ii" and "iii" above shall not apply to current news periodicals and newspapers and current news sections of other periodicals.)

III. Prohibitions as to I and II Above

Notwithstanding any of the above, the following shall be prohibited:

A. Copying shall not be used to create or to replace or substitute for anthologies, compilations or collective works. Such replacement or substitution may occur whether copies of various works or excerpts therefrom are accumulated or reproduced and used separately.

B.	There shall be no copying of or from works intended to be "consumable" in the course of study or of teaching. These include workbooks, exercises, standardized tests and test booklets and answer sheets and like consumable material.

C.	Copying shall not:

    a.	substitute for the purchase of books, publishers' reprints or periodicals;

    b.	be directed by higher authority;

    c.	be repeated with respect to the same item by the same teacher from term to term.

D.	No charge shall be made to the student beyond the actual cost of the photocopying.

Agreed MARCH 19, 1976.

Ad Hoc Committee on Copyright Law Revision by SHELDON ELLIOTT STEINBACH.

Author-Publisher Group and Authors League of America by IRWIN KARP, Counsel.

Association of American Publishers, Inc. by ALEXANDER C. HOFFMAN, Chairman, Copyright Committee.

APPENDIX C
Guidelines for Educational Uses of Music

The purpose of the following guidelines is to state the minimum and not the maximum standards of educational fair use under Section 107 of H.R. 2223. The parties agree that the conditions determining the extent of permissible copying for educational purposes may change in the future; that certain types of copying permitted under these guidelines may not be permissible in the future, and conversely that in the future other types of copying not permitted under these guidelines may be permissible under revised guidelines.

Moreover, the following statement of guidelines is not intended to limit the types of copying permitted under the standards of fair use under judicial decision and which are stated in Section 107 of the Copyright Revision Bill. There may be instances in which copying which does not fall within the guidelines stated below may nonetheless be permitted under the criteria of fair use.

A. Permissible Uses

1. Emergency copying to replace purchased copies which for any reason are not available for an imminent performance provided purchased replacement copies shall be substituted in due course.

2. For academic purposes other than performance, single or multiple copies of excerpts of works may be made, provided that the excerpts do not comprise a part of the whole which would constitute a performable unit such as a section, movement or aria, but in no case more than 10 percent of the whole work. The number of copies shall not exceed one copy per pupil.

3. Printed copies which have been purchased may be edited or simplified provided that the fundamental character of the work is not distorted or the lyrics, if any, altered or lyrics added if none exist.

4. A single copy of recordings of performances by students may be made for evaluation or rehearsal purposes and may be retained by the educational institution or individual teacher.

5. A single copy of a sound recording (such as a tape, disc, or cassette) of copyrighted music may be made from sound recordings owned by an educational institution or an individual teacher for the purpose of constructing aural exercises or examinations and may be retained by the educational institution or individual teacher. (This pertains only to the copyright of the music itself and not to any copyright which may exist in the sound recording.)

B. Prohibitions
1. Copying to create or replace or substitute for anthologies, compilations or collective works.
2. Copying of or from works intended to be "consumable" in the course of study or of teaching such as workbooks, exercises, standardized tests and answer sheets and like material.
3. Copying for the purpose of performance, except as in A(1) above.
4. Copying for the purpose of substituting for the purchase of music, except as in A(1) and A(2) above.
5. Copying without inclusion of the copyright notice which appears on the printed copy.

These guidelines were developed and approved in April 1976 by the Music Publishers' Association of the United States, Inc., the National Music Publishers' Association, Inc., the Music Teachers National Association, the Music Educators National Conference, the National Association of Schools of Music, and the Ad Hoc Committee on Copyright Law Revision.

APPENDIX D
Guidelines for Off-Air Recording of Broadcast Programming for Educational Purposes

In March 1979, Congressman Robert Kastenmeier, Chairman of the House Subcommittee on Courts, Civil Liberties, and Administration of Justice, appointed a Negotiating Committee consisting of representatives of educational organizations, copyright proprietors, and creative guilds and unions. The following guidelines reflect the Negotiating Committee's consensus as to the application of "fair use" to the recording, retention, and use of television broadcast programs for educational purposes. They specify periods of retention and use of such off-air recordings in classrooms and similar places devoted to instruction and for homebound instruction. The purpose of establishing these guidelines is to provide standards for both owners and users of copyrighted television programs.

1. The guidelines were developed to apply only to off-air recording by nonprofit educational institutions.
2. A broadcast program may be recorded off-air simultaneously with broadcast transmission (including simultaneous cable transmission) and retained by a nonprofit educational institution for a period not to exceed the first forty-five (45) consecutive calendar days after date of recording. Upon conclusion of such retention period, all off-air recordings must be erased or destroyed immediately. "Broadcast programs" are television programs transmitted by television stations for reception by the general public without charge.
3. Off-air recordings may be used once by individual teachers in the course of relevant teaching activities, and repeated once only when instructional reinforcement is necessary, in classrooms and similar places devoted to instruction within a single building, cluster or campus, as well as in the homes of students receiving formalized home instruction, during the first ten (10) consecutive school days in the forty-five (45) calendar day retention period. "School days" are school session days—not counting weekends, holidays, vacations, examination periods, or other scheduled interruptions—within the forty-five (45) calendar day retention period.
4. Off-air recordings may be made only at the request of, and used by, individual teachers, and may not be regularly recorded in anticipation of requests. No broadcast program may be recorded off-air more than once at the request of the same teacher, regardless of the number of times the program may be broadcast.

5. A limited number of copies may be reproduced from each off-air recording to meet the legitimate needs of teachers under these guidelines. Each such additional copy shall be subject to all provisions governing the original recording.

6. After the first ten (10) consecutive school days, off-air recording may be used up to the end of the forty-five (45) calendar day retention period only for teacher evaluation purposes, i.e., to determine whether or not to include the broadcast program in the teaching curriculum, and may not be used in the recording institution for student exhibition or any other non-evaluation purpose without authorization.

7. Off-air recordings need not be used in their entirety, but the recorded programs may not be altered from their original content. Off-air recordings may not be physically or electronically combined or merged to constitute teaching anthologies or compilations.

8. All copies of off-air recordings must include the copyright notice on the broadcast program as recorded.

9. Educational institutions are expected to establish appropriate control procedures to maintain the integrity of these guidelines.

APPENDIX E
Model Policy Concerning College and University Photocopying for Classroom, Research, and Library Reserve Use

This model policy, another in a series of copyright advisory documents developed by the American Library Association (ALA), is intended for the guidance and use of academic librarians, faculty, administrators, and legal counsel in response to implementation of the rights and responsibilities provisions of Public Law 94-553, General Revision of the Copyright Law, which took effect on January 1, 1978.

Prepared by ALA Legal Counsel Mary Hutchings of the law firm Sidley & Austin, with advice and assistance from the Copyright Subcommittee (ad hoc) of ALA's Legislation Committee, Association of College and Research Libraries (ACRL) Copyright Committee, Association of Research Libraries (ARL) and other academic librarians and copyright attorneys, the model policy outlines "fair use" rights in the academic environment for classroom teaching, research activities and library services. Please note that it does not address other library photocopying which may be permitted under other sections of the Copyright Law, e.g., Section 108 (Reproduction by Libraries and Archives).

Too often, members of the academic community have been reluctant or hesitant to exercise their rights of fair use under the law for fear of courting an infringement suit. It is important to understand that in U.S. law, copyright is a limited statutory monopoly and the public's right to use materials must be protected. Safeguards have been written into the legislative history accompanying the new copyright law protecting librarians, teachers, researchers and scholars and guaranteeing their rights of access to information as they carry out their responsibilities for educating or conducting research. It is, therefore, important to heed the advice of a former U.S. Register of Copyrights: "If you don't use fair use, you will lose it!"

I. The Copyright Act and Photocopying

From time to time, the faculty and staff of this University [College] may use photocopied materials to supplement research and teaching. In many cases, photocopying can facilitate the University's [College's] mission; that is, the development and transmission of information. However, the photocopying of copyrighted materials is a right granted under the copyright law's doctrine of "fair use" which must not be abused. This report will explain the University's [College's] policy concerning the photocopying of copyrighted materials by faculty and library staff. Please note that this policy does not address other library photocopying which may be permitted under sections of the copyright law, e.g., 17 U.S.C. § 108.

Copyright is a constitutionally conceived property right which is designed to promote the progress of science and the useful arts by securing for an author the benefits of his or her original work of authorship for a limited time. U.S. Constitution, Art. I, Sec. 8. The Copyright statute, 17 U.S.C. § 101 et seq., implements this policy by balancing the author's interest against the public interest in the dissemination of information affecting areas of universal concern, such as art, science, history and business. The grand design of this delicate balance is to foster the creation and dissemination of intellectual works for the general public.

The Copyright Act defines the rights of a copyright holder and how they may be enforced against an infringer. Included within the Copyright Act is the "fair use" doctrine which allows, under certain conditions, the copying of copyrighted material. While the Act lists general factors under the heading of "fair use" it provides little in the way of specific directions for what constitutes fair use. The law states:

17 U.S.C. § 107. Limitations on exclusive rights: Fair use
Notwithstanding the provisions of section 106, the fair use of a copyrighted work, including such use by reproduction in copies or phonorecords or by any other means specified by that section, for purposes such as criticism, comment, news reporting, teaching (including multiple copies for classroom use), scholarship, or research, is not an infringement of copyright. In determining whether the use made of a work in any particular case is a fair use the factors to be considered shall include—
(1)   the purpose and character of the use, including whether such use is of a commercial nature or is for nonprofit educational purposes;
(2)   the nature of copyrighted work;
(3)   the amount and substantiality of the portion used in relation to the copyrighted work as a whole; and
(4)   the effect of the use upon the potential market for or value of the copyrighted work.

The purpose of this report is to provide you, the faculty and staff of this University [College], with an explanation of when the photocopying of copyrighted material in our opinion is permitted under the fair use doctrine. Where possible, common examples of research, classroom, and library reserve photocopying have been included to illustrate what we believe to be the reach and limits of fair use.

Please note that the copyright law applies to all forms of photocopying, whether it is undertaken at a commercial copying center, at the University's [College's] central or departmental copying facilities or at a self-service machine. While you are free to use the services of a commercial establishment, you should be prepared to provide documentation of permission from the publisher (if such permission is necessary under this policy), since many commercial copiers will require such proof.

We hope this report will give you an appreciation of the factors which weigh in favor of fair use and those factors which weigh against fair use, but faculty members must determine for themselves which works will be photocopied. This University [College] does not condone a policy of photocopying instead of purchasing copyrighted works where such photocopying would constitute an infringement under the Copyright law, but it does encourage faculty members to exercise good judgment in serving the best interests of students in an efficient manner.

Instructions for securing permission to photocopy copyrighted works when such copying is beyond the limits of fair use appear at the end of this report. It is the policy of this University that the user (faculty, staff or librarian) secure such permission whenever it is legally necessary.

II. Unrestricted Photocopying

A. Uncopyrighted Published Works

Writing published before January 1, 1978 which has never been copyrighted may be photocopied without restriction. Copies of works protected by copyright must bear a copyright notice, which consists of the letter "c" in a circle, or the word "Copyright," or the abbreviation "Copr.," plus the year of first publication, plus the name of the copyright owner. 17 U.S.C. § 401. As to works published before January 1, 1978, in the case of a book, the notice must be placed on the title page or the reverse side of the title page. In the case of a periodical the notice must be placed either on the title page, the first page of text, or in the masthead. A pre-1978 failure to comply with the notice requirements results in the work being injected into the public domain, i.e., unprotected. Copyright notice requirements have been relaxed since 1978, so that the absence of notice on copies of a work published after January 1, 1978 does not necessarily mean the work is in the public domain. 17 U.S.C. § 405(a) and (c). However, you will not be liable for damages for copyright infringement of works published after that date, if, after normal inspection, you photocopy a work on which you cannot find a copyright symbol and you have not received actual notice of the fact the work is copyrighted. 17 U.S.C. § 405(b). However, a copyright owner who found out about your photocopying would have the right to prevent further distribution of the copies if in fact the work were copyrighted and the copies are infringing. 17 U.S.C. § 405(b).

B. Published Works with Expired Copyrights

Writings with expired copyrights may be photocopied without restriction. All copyrights prior to 1906 have expired. 17 U.S.C. § 304(b). Copyrights granted after 1906 may have been renewed; however the writing will probably not contain notice of the renewal. Therefore, it should be assumed all writings dated 1906 or later are covered by a valid copyright, unless information to the contrary is obtained from the owner or the U.S. Copyright Office (see Copyright Office Circular 15t).

Copyright Office Circular R22 explains how to investigate the copyright status of a work. One way is to use the Catalog of Copyright Entries published by the Copyright

Office and available in [the University Library] many libraries. Alternatively you may request the Copyright Office to conduct a search of its registration and/or assignment records. The Office charges an hourly fee for this service. You will need to submit as much information as you have concerning the work in which you are interested, such as the title, author, approximate date of publication, the type of work or any available copyright data. The Copyright Office does caution that its searches are not conclusive; for instance, if a work obtained copyright less than 28 years ago, it may be fully protected although there has been no registration or deposit.

C. Unpublished Works

Unpublished works, such as theses and dissertations, may be protected by copyright. If such a work was created before January 1, 1978 and has not been copyrighted or published without copyright notice, the work is protected under the new Act for the life of the author plus fifty years, 17 U.S.C. § 303, but in no case earlier than December 31, 2002. If such a work is published on or before that date, the copyright will not expire before December 31, 2027. Works created after January 1, 1978 and not published enjoy copyright protection for the life of the author plus fifty years. 17 U.S.C. § 302.

D. U.S. Government Publications

All U.S. Government publications with the possible exception of some National Technical Information Service Publications less than five years old may be photocopied without restrictions, except to the extent they contain copyrighted materials from other sources. 17 U.S.C. § 105. U.S. Government publications are documents prepared by an official or employee of the government in an official capacity. 17 U.S.C. § 101. Government publications include the opinions of courts in legal cases, Congressional Reports on proposed bills, testimony offered at Congressional hearings and the works of government employees in their official capacities. Works prepared by outside authors on contract to the government may or may not be protected by copyright, depending on the specifics of the contract. In the absence of copyright notice on such works, it would be reasonable to assume they are government works in the public domain. It should be noted that state government works may be protected by copyright. See, 17 U.S.C. § 105. However, the opinions of state courts are not protected.

III. Permissible Photocopying of Copyrighted Works

The Copyright Act allows anyone to photocopy copyrighted works without securing permission from the copyright owner when the photocopying amounts to a "fair use" of the material. 17 U.S.C. § 107. The guidelines in this report discuss the boundaries for fair use of photocopied material used in research or the classroom or in a library reserve operation. Fair use cannot always be expressed in numbers—either the number of pages copied or the number of copies distributed. Therefore, you should weigh the various factors listed in the Act and judge whether the intended use of photocopied, copyrighted material is within the spirit of the fair use doctrine. Any serious questions concerning whether a particular photocopying constitutes fair use should be directed to University [College] counsel.

A. Research Uses

At the very least, instructors may make a single copy of any of the following for scholarly research or use in teaching or preparing to teach a class:

1. a chapter from a book;
2. an article from a periodical or newspaper;
3. a short story, short essay, or short poem, whether or not from a collective work;
4. a chart, diagram, graph, drawing, cartoon or picture from a book, periodical, or newspaper.

These examples reflect the most conservative guidelines for fair use. They do not represent inviolate ceilings for the amount of copyrighted material which can be photocopied within the boundaries of fair use. When exceeding these minimum levels, however, you again should consider the four factors listed in Section 107 of the Copyright Act to make sure that any additional photocopying is justified. The following demonstrate situations where increased levels of photocopying would continue to remain within the ambit of fair use:

1. the inability to obtain another copy of the work because it is not available from another library or source cannot be obtained within your time constraints;
2. the intention to photocopy the material only once and not to distribute the material to others;
3. the ability to keep the amount of material photocopied within a reasonable proportion to the entire work (the larger the work, the greater amount of material which may be photocopied).

Most single-copy photocopying for your personal use in research—even when it involves a substantial portion of a work—may well constitute fair use.

B. Classroom Uses

Primary and secondary school educators have, with publishers, developed the following guidelines, which allow a teacher to distribute photocopied material to students in a class without the publisher's prior permission, under the following conditions:

1. the distribution of the same photocopied material does not occur every semester;
2. only one copy is distributed for each student which copy must become the student's property;
3. the material includes a copyright notice on the first page of the portion of material photocopied;
4. the students are not assessed any fee beyond the actual cost of the photocopying.

In addition, the educators agreed that the amount of material distributed should not exceed certain brevity standards. Under those guidelines, a prose work may be reproduced in its entirety if it is less than 2500 words in length. If the work exceeds such length, the excerpt reproduced may not exceed 1000 words, or 10% of the work, whichever is less. In the case of poetry, 250 words is the maximum permitted.

These minimum standards normally would not be realistic in the University setting. Faculty members needing to exceed these limits for college education should not feel hampered by these guidelines, although they should attempt a "selective and sparing" use of photocopied, copyrighted material.

The photocopying practices of an instructor should not have a significant detrimental impact on the market for the copyrighted work. 17 U.S.C. § 107(4). To guard against this effect, you usually should restrict use of an item of photocopied material to one course and you should not repeatedly photocopy excerpts from one periodical or author without the permission of the copyright owner.

C. Library Reserve Uses

At the request of a faculty member, a library may photocopy and place on reserve excerpts from copyrighted works in its collection in accordance with guidelines similar to those governing formal classroom distribution for face-to-face teaching discussed above. This University [College] believes that these guidelines apply to the library reserve shelf to the extent it functions as an extension of classroom readings or reflects an individual student's right to photocopy for his personal scholastic use under the doctrine of fair use. In general, librarians may photocopy materials for reserve room use for the convenience of students both in preparing class assignments and in pursuing informal educational activities which higher education requires, such as advanced independent study and research.

If the request calls for only one copy to be placed on reserve, the library may photocopy an entire article, or an entire chapter from a book, or an entire poem. Requests for multiple copies on reserve should meet the following guidelines:

1. the amount of material should be reasonable in relation to the total amount of material assigned for one term of a course taking into account the nature of the course, its subject matter and level, 17 U.S.C. § 107(1) and (3);
2. the number of copies should be reasonable in light of the number of students enrolled, the difficulty and timing of assignments, and the number of other courses which may assign the same material, 17 U.S.C. § 107(1) and (3);
3. the material should contain a notice of copyright, see 17 U.S.C. § 401;
4. the effect of photocopying the material should not be detrimental to the market for the work. (In general, the library should own at least one copy of the work.) 17 U.S.C. § 107(4).

For example, a professor may place on reserve as a supplement to the course textbook a reasonable number of copies of articles from academic journals or chapters from trade books. A reasonable number of copies will in most instances be less than six, but factors such as the length or difficulty of the assignment, the number of enrolled students and the length of time allowed for completion of the assignment may permit more in unusual circumstances.

In addition, a faculty member may also request that multiple copies of photocopied, copyrighted material be placed on the reserve shelf if there is insufficient time to obtain permission from the copyright owner. For example, a professor may place on reserve several photocopies of an entire article from a recent issue of *Time* magazine or the *New York Times* in lieu of distributing a copy to each member of the class. If you are in doubt as to whether a particular instance of photocopying is fair use in the reserve reading room, you should waive any fee for such a use.

D. Uses of Photocopied Material Requiring Permission

1. repetitive copying: The classroom or reserve use of photocopied materials in multiple courses or successive years will normally require advance permission from the owner of the copyright, 17 U.S.C. § 107(3).

2. copying for profit: Faculty should not charge students more than the actual cost of photocopying the material, 17 U.S.C. § 107(1).

3. consumable works: The duplication of works that are consumed in the classroom, such as standardized tests, exercises, and workbooks, normally requires permission from the copyright owner, 17 U.S.C. § 107(4).

4. creation of anthologies as basic text material for a course: Creation of a collective work or anthology by photocopying a number of copyrighted articles and excerpts to be purchased and used together as the basic text for a course will in most instances require the permission of the copyrighted owners. Such photocopying of a book is thus less likely to be deemed fair use, 17 U.S.C. § 107(4).

E. How to Obtain Permission

When a use of photocopied material requires that you request permission, you should communicate complete and accurate information to the copyright owner. The American Association of Publishers suggests that the following information be included in a permission request letter in order to expedite the process:

1. Title, author and/or editor, and edition of materials to be duplicated.

2. Exact material to be used, giving amount, page numbers, chapters and, if possible, a photocopy of the material.

3. Number of copies to be made.

4. Use to be made of duplicated materials.

5. Form of distribution (classroom, newsletter, etc.).

6. Whether or not the material is to be sold.

7. Type of reprint (ditto, photography, offset, typeset).

The request should be sent, together with a self-addressed return envelope, to the permissions department of the publisher in question. If the address of the publisher does not appear at the front of the material, it may be readily obtained in a publication entitled *The Literary Marketplace*, published by the R. R. Bowker Company and available in all libraries.

The process of granting permission requires time for the publisher to check the status of the copyright and to evaluate the nature of the request. It is advisable, therefore, to allow enough lead time to obtain permission before the materials are needed. In some instances, the publisher may assess a fee for the permission. It is not inappropriate to pass this fee on to the students who receive copies of the photocopied material.

The Copyright Clearance Center also has the right to grant permission and collect fees for photocopying rights for certain publications. Libraries may copy from any journal which is registered with the CCC and report the copying beyond fair use to CCC and pay the set fee. A list of publications for which the CCC handles fees and permissions is available from CCC, 310 Madison Avenue, New York, NY 10017.

Sample Letter to Copyright Owner (Publisher) Requesting Permission to Copy

March 1, 1982

Material Permissions Department
Hypothetical Book Company
500 East Avenue
Chicago, IL 60601

Dear Sir or Madam:

I would like permission to copy the following for continued use in my classes in future semesters:

Title: Learning Is Good, Second Edition
Copyright: Hypothetical Book Co., 1965, 1971
Author: Frank Jones
Material to be duplicated: Chapters 10, 11 and 14 (photocopy enclosed)
Number of copies: 500
Distribution: The material will be distributed to students in my classes and they will pay only the cost of the photocopying.
Type of reprint: Photocopy
Use: The chapters will be used as supplementary teaching materials.

I have enclosed a self-addressed envelope for your convenience in replying to this request.

Sincerely,
Faculty Member

F. Infringement

Courts and legal scholars alike have commented that the fair use provisions in the Copyright Act are among the most vague and difficult that can be found anywhere in the law. In amending the Copyright Act in 1976, Congress anticipated the problem this would pose for users of copyrighted materials who wished to stay under the umbrella of protection offered by fair use. For this reason, the Copyright Act contains specific provisions which grant additional rights to libraries and insulate employees of a non-profit educational institution, library, or archives from statutory damages for infringement where the infringer believed or had reasonable ground to believe the photocopying was a fair use of the material. 17 U.S.C. § 504(c)(2).

Normally, an infringer is liable to the copyright owner for the actual losses sustained because of the photocopying and any additional profits of the infringer. 17 U.S.C. § 504(a)(1) and (b). Where the monetary losses are nominal, the copyright owner usually will claim statutory damages instead of the actual losses. 17 U.S.C. § 504(a)(2) and (c). The statutory damages may reach as high as $10,000 (or up to $50,000 if the infringement is willful). In addition to suing for money damages, a copyright owner can usually prevent future infringement through a court injunction. 17 U.S.C. § 502.

The Copyright Act specifically exempts from statutory damages any employee of a non-profit educational institution, library, or archives, who "believed and had reasonable grounds for believing that his or her use of the copyrighted work was a fair use under Section 107." 17 U.S.C. § 504(c)(2). While the fair use provisions are admittedly ambiguous, any employee who attempts to stay within the guidelines contained in this report should have an adequate good faith defense in the case of an innocently committed infringement.

If the criteria contained in this report are followed, it is our view that no copyright infringement will occur and that there will be no adverse effect on the market for copyrighted works.

(Many educational institutions will provide their employees legal counsel without charge if an infringement suit is brought against the employee for photocopying performed in the course of employment. If so, this should be noted here.)

Source: Model Policy Concerning College and University Photocopying for Classroom, Research and Library Reserve Use, American Library Association, Washington Office, Washington, DC, March 1982. ISBN: 0-9389-5624.

APPENDIX F
CONTU Guidelines on Photocopying under Interlibrary Loan Arrangements

The CONTU guidelines were developed to assist librarians and copyright proprietors in understanding the amount of photocopying for use in interlibrary loan arrangements permitted under the copyright law. In the spring of 1976 there was realistic expectation that a new copyright law, under consideration for nearly twenty years, would be enacted during that session of Congress. It had become apparent that the House subcommittee was giving serious consideration to modifying the language concerning "systematic reproduction" by libraries in Section 108(g)(2) of the Senate-passed bill to permit photocopying under interlibrary arrangements, unless such arrangements resulted in the borrowing libraries obtaining "such aggregate quantities as to substitute for a subscription to or purchase of" copyrighted works.

The Commission discussed this proposed amendment to the Senate bill at its meeting on April 2, 1976. Pursuant to a request made at that meeting by the Register of Copyrights, serving in her *ex officio* role, the Commission agreed that it might aid the House and Senate subcommittees by offering its good offices in bringing the principal parties together to see whether agreement could be reached on a definition of "such aggregate quantities." This offer was accepted by the House and Senate subcommittees and the interested parties, and much of the summer of 1976 was spent by the Commission in working with the parties to secure agreement on "guidelines" interpreting what was to become the proviso in Section 108(g)(2) relating to "systematic reproduction" by libraries. The pertinent parts of that section, with the proviso added by the House emphasized, follow:

> (g) The rights of reproduction and distribution under this section extend to the isolated and unrelated reproduction or distribution of a single copy or phonorecord of the same material on separate occasions, but do not extend to cases where the library or archives, or its employee . . .
> (2) engages in the systematic reproduction or distribution of single or multiple copies or phonorecords of material described in subsection (d): *Provided, That nothing in this clause prevents a library or archives from participating in interlibrary arrangements that do not have, as their purpose or effect, that the library or archives receiving such copies or phonorecords for distribution does so in such aggregate quantities as to substitute for a subscription to or purchase of such work.*

Before enactment of the new copyright law, the principal library, publisher, and author organizations agreed to the following detailed guidelines defining what "aggregate quantities" would constitute the "systematic reproduction" that would exceed the statutory limitations on a library's photocopying activities.

PHOTOCOPYING—INTERLIBRARY ARRANGEMENTS

Introduction

Subsection 108(g)(2) of the bill deals, among other things, with limits on interlibrary arrangements for photocopying. It prohibits systematic photocopying of copyrighted materials but permits interlibrary arrangements "that do not have, as their purpose or effect, that the library or archives receiving such copies or phonorecords for distribution does so in such aggregate quantities as to substitute for a subscription to or purchase of such work."

The National Commission on New Technological Uses of Copyrighted Works offered its good offices to the House and Senate subcommittees in bringing the interested parties together to see if agreement could be reached on what a realistic definition would be of "such aggregate quantities." The Commission consulted with the parties and suggested the interpretation which follows, on which there has been substantial agreement by the principal library, publisher, and author organizations. The Commission considers the guidelines which follow to be a workable and fair interpretation of the intent of the proviso portion of subsection 108(g)(2).

These guidelines are intended to provide guidance in the application of section 108 to the most frequently encountered interlibrary case: a library's obtaining from another library, in lieu of interlibrary loan, copies of articles from relatively recent issues of periodicals—those published within five years prior to the date of the request. The guidelines do not specify what aggregate quantity of copies of an article or articles published in a periodical, the issue date of which is more than five years prior to the date when the request for the copy thereof is made, constitutes a substitute for a subscription to such periodical. The meaning of the proviso to subsection 108(g)(2) in such case is left to future interpretation.

The point has been made that the present practice on interlibrary loans and use of photocopies in lieu of loans may be supplemented or even largely replaced by a system in which one or more agencies or institutions, public or private, exist for the specific purpose of providing a central source for photocopies. Of course, these guidelines would not apply to such a situation.

Guidelines for the Proviso of Subsection 108(g)(2)

1. As used in the proviso of subsection 108(g)(2), the words ". . . such aggregate quantities as to substitute for a subscription to or purchase of such work" shall mean:
    (a) with respect to any given periodical (as opposed to any given issue of a periodical), filled requests of a library or archives (a "requesting entity") within any calendar

year for a total of six or more copies of an article or articles published in such periodical within five years prior to the date of the request. These guidelines specifically shall not apply, directly or indirectly, to any request of a requesting entity for a copy or copies of an article or articles published in any issue of a periodical, the publication date of which is more than five years prior to the date when the request is made. These guidelines do not define the meaning, with respect to such a request, of ". . . such aggregate quantities as to substitute for a subscription to [such periodical]."

(b) With respect to any other material described in subsection 108(d), including fiction and poetry, filled requests of a requesting entity within any calendar year for a total of six or more copies or phonorecords of or from any given work (including a collective work) during the entire period when such material shall be protected by copyright.

2. In the event that a requesting entity:

(a) shall have in force or shall have entered an order for a subscription to a periodical, or

(b) has within its collection, or shall have entered an order for, a copy or phonorecord of any other copyrighted work, material from either category of which it desires to obtain by copy from another library or archives (the "supplying entity"), because the material to be copied is not reasonably available for use by the requesting entity itself, then the fulfillment of such request shall be treated as though the requesting entity made such copy from its own collection. A library or archives may request a copy or phonorecord from a supplying entity only under those circumstances where the requesting entity would have been able, under the other provisions of section 108, to supply such copy from materials in its own collection.

3. No request for a copy or phonorecord of any material to which these guidelines apply may be fulfilled by the supplying entity unless such request is accompanied by a representation by the requesting entity that the request was made in conformity with these guidelines.

4. The requesting entity shall maintain records of all requests made by it for copies or phonorecords of any materials to which these guidelines apply and shall maintain records of the fulfillment of such requests, which records shall be retained until the end of the third complete calendar year after the end of the calendar year in which the respective request shall have been made.

5. As part of the review provided for in subsection 108(i), these guidelines shall be reviewed not later than five years from the effective date of this bill.

These guidelines were accepted by the Conference Committee and were incorporated into its report on the new act. During the ensuing twenty months, both library and publisher organizations have reported considerable progress toward adapting their practices to conform with the CONTU guidelines.

The guidelines specifically leave the status of periodical articles more than five years old to future determination. Moreover, institutions set up for the specific purpose of supplying photocopies of copyrighted material are excluded from coverage of the guidelines.

Source: Final Report of the National Commission on New Technological Uses of Copyrighted Works, July 31, 1978, Library of Congress, Washington, DC, 1979, pages 54–55.

APPENDIX G
Fair Use Guidelines for Educational Multimedia*

1. **Introduction**
   1.1 **Preamble**

   Fair use is a legal principle that defines the limitations on the exclusive rights** of copyright holders. The purpose of these guidelines is to provide guidance on the application of fair use principles by educators, scholars and students who develop multimedia projects using portions of copyrighted works under fair use rather than by seeking authorization for non-commercial educational uses. These guidelines apply only to fair use in the context of copyright and to no other rights.

   There is no simple test to determine what is fair use. Section 107 of the Copyright Act*** sets forth the four fair use factors which should be considered in each instance, based on particular facts of a given case, to determine whether a use is a "fair use": (1) the purpose and character of use, including whether such use is of a commercial nature or is for nonprofit educational purposes, (2) the nature of the copyrighted work, (3) the amount and substantiality of the portion used in relation to the copyrighted work as a whole, and (4) the effect of the use upon the potential market for or value of the copyrighted work.

   While only the courts can authoritatively determine whether a particular use is fair use, these guidelines represent the participants'**** consensus of conditions under which fair use should generally apply and examples of when permission is required. Uses that exceed these guidelines may nor may not be fair use. The participants also agree that the more one exceeds these guidelines, the greater the risk that fair use does not apply.

   The limitations and conditions set forth in these guidelines do not apply to works in the public domain—such as U.S. Government works or works on which

---

*These Guidelines shall not be read to supersede other preexisting education fair use guidelines that deal with the Copyright Act of 1976.

**See Section 106 of the Copyright Act.

***The Copyright Act of 1976, as amended, is codified at 17 U.S.C. § 101 et seq.

****The names of the various organizations participating in this dialog appear at the end of these guidelines and clearly indicate the variety of interest groups involved, both from the standpoint of the users of copyrighted material and also from the standpoint of the copyright owners.

copyright has expired for which there are no copyright restrictions—or to works for which the individual or institution has obtained permission for the particular use. Also, license agreements may govern the uses of some works and users should refer to the applicable license terms for guidance.

The participants who developed these guidelines met for an extended period of time and the result represents their collective understanding in this complex area. Because digital technology is in a dynamic phase, there may come a time when it is necessary to review the guidelines. Nothing in these guidelines shall be construed to apply to the fair use privilege in any context outside of educational and scholarly uses of educational multimedia projects.

This Preamble is an integral part of these guidelines and should be included whenever the guidelines are reprinted or adopted by organizations and educational institutions. Users are encouraged to reproduce and distribute these guidelines freely without permission; no copyright protection of these guidelines is claimed by any person or entity.

1.2 Background

These guidelines clarify the application of fair use of copyrighted works as teaching methods are adapted to new learning environments. Educators have traditionally brought copyrighted books, videos, slides, sound recordings and other media into the classroom, along with accompanying projection and playback equipment. Multimedia creators integrated these individual instructional resources with their own original works in a meaningful way, providing compact educational tools that allow great flexibility in teaching and learning. Material is stored so that it may be retrieved in a nonlinear fashion, depending on the needs or interests of learners. Educators can use multimedia projects to respond spontaneously to students' questions by referring quickly to relevant portions. In addition, students can use multimedia projects to pursue independent study according to their needs or at a pace appropriate to their capabilities. Educators and students want guidance about the application of fair use principles when creating their own multimedia projects to meet specific instructional objectives.

1.3 Applicability of These Guidelines

These guidelines apply to the use, without permission, of portions of lawfully acquired copyrighted works in educational multimedia projects which are created by educators or students as part of a systematic learning activity by nonprofit educational institutions.

Educational multimedia projects created under these guidelines incorporate students' or educators' original material, such as course notes or commentary, together with various copyrighted media formats including but not limited to, motion media, music, text material, graphics, illustrations, photographs and digital software which are combined into an integrated presentation. Educational institutions are defined as nonprofit organizations whose primary focus is supporting research and instructional activities of educators and students for noncommercial purposes.

For the purposes of the guidelines, educators include faculty, teachers, instructors, and others who engage in scholarly, research and instructional activities for educational institutions. The copyrighted works used under these guidelines are lawfully acquired if obtained by the institution or individual through lawful means such as purchase, gift or license agreement but not pirated copies. Educational multimedia projects which incorporate portions of copyrighted works under these guidelines may be used only for educational purposes in systematic learning activities including use in connection with non-commercial curriculum-based learning and teaching activities by educators to students enrolled in courses at nonprofit educational institutions or otherwise permitted under Section 3. While these guidelines refer to the creation and use of educational multimedia projects, readers are advised that in some instances other fair use guidelines such as those for off-air taping may be relevant.

2. Preparation of Educational Multimedia Projects Using Portions of Copyrighted Works

These uses are subject to the Portion Limitations listed in Section 4. They should include proper attribution and citation as defined in Section 6.2.

2.1 By Students:

Students may incorporate portions of lawfully acquired copyrighted works when producing their own educational multimedia projects for a specific course.

2.2 By Educators for Curriculum-Based Instruction:

Educators may incorporate portions of lawfully acquired copyrighted works when producing their own educational multimedia programs for their own teaching tools in support of curriculum-based instructional activities at educational institutions.

3. Permitted Uses of Educational Multimedia Programs Created under These Guidelines

Uses of educational multimedia projects created under these guidelines are subject to the Time, Portion, Copying and Distribution Limitations listed in Section 4.

3.1 Student Use:

Students may perform and display their own educational multimedia projects created under Section 2 of these guidelines for educational uses in the course for which they were created and may use them in their own portfolios as examples of their academic work for later personal uses such as job and graduate school interviews.

3.2 Educator Use for Curriculum-Based Instruction:

Educators may perform and display their own educational multimedia projects created under Section 2 for curriculum-based instruction to students in the following situations:

3.2.1   for face-to-face instruction,

3.2.2   assigned to students for directed self-study,

3.2.3   for remote instruction to students enrolled in curriculum-based courses and located at remote sites, provided over the educational institution's secure electronic network in real-time, or for after class review or directed self-study, provided there are technological limitations on access to the network and educational multimedia project (such as a password or PIN) and provided further that the technology prevents the making of copies of copyrighted material.

If the educational institution's network or technology used to access the educational multimedia project created under Section 2 of these guidelines cannot prevent duplication of copyrighted material, students or educators may use the multimedia educational projects over an otherwise secure network for a period of only 15 days after its initial real-time remote use in the course of instruction or 15 days after its assignment for directed self-study. After that period, one of the two use copies of the educational multimedia project may be placed on reserve in a learning resource center, library or similar facility for on-site use by students enrolled in the course. Students shall be advised that they are not permitted to make their own copies of the multimedia project.

3.3 Educator Use for Peer Conferences:

Educators may perform or display their own multimedia projects created under Section 2 of these guidelines in presentations to their peers, for example, at workshops and conferences.

3.4 Educator Use for Professional Portfolio

Educators may retain educational multimedia projects created under Section 2 of these guidelines in their personal portfolios for later personal uses such as tenure review or job interviews.

4.   Limitations—Time, Portion, Copying and Distribution

The preparation of educational multimedia projects incorporating copyrighted works under Section 2, and the use of such projects under Section 3, are subject to the limitations noted below.

4.1 Time Limitations

Educators may use their educational multimedia projects created for educational purposes under Section 2 of these guidelines for teaching courses, for a period of up to two years after the first instructional use with a class. Use beyond that time period, even for educational purposes, requires permission for each copyrighted portion incorporated in the production. Students may use their educational multimedia projects as noted in Section 3.1.

4.2 Portion Limitations

Portion limitations mean the amount of a copyrighted work that can reasonably be used in educational multimedia projects under these guidelines regardless of the original medium from which the copyrighted works are taken. In the aggregate means the total amount of copyrighted material from a single copyrighted work that is permitted to be used in an educational multimedia project without permission under these guidelines. These limits apply cumulatively to each educator's or student's multimedia project(s) for the same academic semester, cycle or term. All students should be instructed about the reasons for copyright protection and the need to follow these guidelines. It is understood, however, that students in kindergarten through grade six may not be able to adhere rigidly to the portion limitations in this section in their independent development of educational multimedia projects. In any event, each such project retained under Sections 3.1 and 4.3 should comply with the portion limitations in this section.

4.2.1 Motion Media

Up to 10% or 3 minutes, whichever is less, in the aggregate of a copyrighted motion media work may be reproduced or otherwise incorporated as part of a multimedia project created under Section 2 of these guidelines.

4.2.2 Text Material

Up to 10% or 1000 words, whichever is less, in the aggregate of a copyrighted work consisting of text material may be reproduced or otherwise incorporated as part of a multimedia project created under Section 2 of these guidelines. An entire poem of less than 250 words may be used, but no more than three poems by one poet, or five poems by different poets from any anthology may be used. For poems of greater length, 250 words may be used but no more than three excerpts by a poet, or five excerpts by different poets from a single anthology may be used.

4.2.3 Music, Lyrics, and Music Video

Up to 10%, but in no event more than 30 seconds, of the music and lyrics from an individual musical work (or in the aggregate of extracts from an individual work), whether the musical work is embodied in copies, or audio or audiovisual works, may be reproduced or otherwise incorporated as a part of a multimedia project created under Section 2. Any alterations to a musical work shall not change the basic melody or the fundamental character of the work.

4.2.4   Illustrations and Photographs

The reproduction or incorporation of photographs and illustrations is more difficult to define with regard to fair use because fair use usually precludes the use of an entire work. Under these guidelines a photograph or illustration may be used in its entirety but no more than 5 images by an artist or photographer may be reproduced or otherwise incorporated as part of an educational multimedia project created under Section 2. When using photographs and illustrations from a published collective work, not more than 10% or 15 images, whichever is less, may be reproduced or otherwise incorporated as part of an educational multimedia project created under Section 2.

4.2.5   Numerical Data Sets

Up to 10% or 2500 fields or cell entries, whichever is less, from a copyrighted database or data table may be reproduced or otherwise incorporated as part of an educational multimedia project created under Section 2 of these guidelines. A field entry is defined as a specific item of information, such as a name or Social Security number, in a record of a database file. A cell entry is defined as the intersection where a row and a column meet on a spreadsheet.

4.3 Copying and Distribution Limitations

Only a limited number of copies, including the original, may be made of an educator's educational multimedia project. For all of the uses permitted by Section 3, there may be no more than two use copies only one of which may be placed on reserve as described in Section 3.2.3.

An additional copy may be made for preservation purposes but may only be used or copied to replace a use copy that has been lost, stolen, or damaged. In the case of a jointly created educational multimedia project, each principal creator may retain one copy but only for the purposes described in Sections 3.3 and 3.4 for educators and Section 3.1 for students.

5.   Examples of When Permission Is Required

5.1 Using Multimedia Projects for Non-Educational or Commercial Purposes

Educators and students must seek individual permissions (licenses) before using copyrighted works in educational multimedia projects for commercial reproduction and distribution.

5.2 Duplication of Multimedia Projects Beyond Limitations Listed in These Guidelines

Even for educational uses, educators and students must seek individual permissions for all copyrighted works incorporated in their personally created educational multimedia projects before replicating or distributing beyond the limitations listed in Section 4.3.

5.3 Distribution of Multimedia Projects beyond Limitations Listed in These Guidelines

Educators and students may not use their personally created educational multimedia projects over electronic networks, except for uses as described in Section 3.2.3, without obtaining permissions for all copyrighted works incorporated in the program.

6. Important Reminders

6.1 Caution in Downloading Material from the Internet

Educators and students are advised to exercise caution in using digital material downloaded from the Internet in producing their own educational multimedia projects, because there is a mix of works protected by copyright and works in the public domain on the network. Access to works on the Internet does not automatically mean that these can be reproduced and reused without permission or royalty payment and, furthermore, some copyrighted works may have been posted to the Internet without authorization of the copyright holder.

6.2 Attribution and Acknowledgement

Educators and students are reminded to credit the sources and display the copyright notice © and copyright ownership information if this is shown in the original source, for all works incorporated as part of the educational multimedia projects prepared by educators and students, including those prepared under fair use. Crediting the source must adequately identify the source of the work, giving a full bibliographic description where available (including author, title, publisher, and place and date of publication). The copyright ownership information includes the copyright notice (©, year of first publication and name of the copyright holder).

The credit and copyright notice information may be combined and shown in a separate section of the educational multimedia project (e.g., credit section) except for images incorporated into the project for the uses described in Section 3.2.3. In such cases, the copyright notice and the name of the creator of the image must be incorporated into the image when, and to the extent, such information is reasonably available; credit and copyright notice information is considered "incorporated" if it is attached to the image file and appears on the screen when the image is viewed. In those cases when displaying source credits and copyright ownership information on the screen with the image would be mutually exclusive with an instructional objective (e.g., during examinations in which the source credits and/or copyright information would be relevant to the examination questions), those images may be displayed without such information being simultaneously displayed on the screen. In such cases, this information should be linked to the image in a manner compatible with such instructional objectives.

6.3 Notice of Use Restrictions

Educators and students are advised that they must include on the opening screen of their multimedia program and any accompanying print material a notice that certain materials are included under the fair use exemption of the U.S. Copyright Law and have been prepared according to the multimedia fair use guidelines and are restricted from further use.

6.4 Future Uses beyond Fair Use

Educators and students are advised to note that if there is a possibility that their own educational multimedia project incorporating copyrighted works under fair use could later result in broader dissemination, whether or not as commercial product, it is strongly recommended that they take steps to obtain permissions during the development process for all copyrighted portions rather than waiting until after completion of the project.

6.5 Integrity of Copyrighted Works: Alterations

Educators and students may make alterations in the portions of the copyrighted works they incorporate as part of an educational multimedia project only if the alterations support specific instructional objectives. Educators and students are advised to note that alterations have been made.

6.6 Reproduction or Decompilation of Copyrighted Computer Programs

Educators and students should be aware that reproduction or decompilation of copyrighted computer programs and portions thereof, for example the transfer of underlying code or control mechanisms, even for educational uses, are outside the scope of these guidelines.

6.7 Licenses and Contracts

Educators and students should determine whether specific copyrighted works, or other data or information are subject to a license or contract. Fair use and these guidelines shall not preempt or supersede licenses and contractual obligations. Being a participant does not necessarily mean that the organization has or will endorse these guidelines.

Agency for Instructional Technology (AIT)
American Association of Community Colleges (AACC)
American Association of Higher Education (AAHE)
American Library Association (ALA)
American Society of Journal Authors, Inc. (ASJA)
American Society of Media Photographers (ASMP)
Artists Rights Foundation
Association of American Colleges and Universities (AAC&U)

Association of American Publishers (AAP)

—Harvard University Press
—Houghton Mifflin
—McGraw-Hill
—Simon and Schuster
—Worth Publishers

Association of College Research Libraries (ACRL)
Association for Educational Communications and Technology (AECT)
Association for Information Media and Equipment (AIME)
Association of Research Libraries (ARL)
Authors Guild, Inc.
Broadcast Music, Inc. (BMI)
Consortium of College and University Media Centers (CCUMC)
Copyright Clearance Center (CCC)
Creative Incentive Coalition (CIC)
Directors Guild of America (DGA)
European American Music Distributors Corp.
Educational institutions represented

—American University
—Carnegie Mellon University
—City College/City University of New York
—Kent State University
—Maricopa Community Colleges/Phoenix
—Penn State University
—University of Delaware

Information Industry Association (IIA)
Instructional Telecommunications Council (ITC)
International Association of Scientific, Technical and Medical Publishers
Motion Picture Association of America (MPAA)
Music Publishers Association (MPA)
National Association of State Universities and Land-Grant Colleges (NASULGC)
National Council of Teachers of Mathematics (NCTM)
National Educational Association (NEA)
National Music Publishers Association (NMPA)
National School Boards Association (NSBA)
National Science Teachers Association (NSTA)
National Video Resources (NVR)

Public Broadcasting System (PBS)
Recording Industry Association of America (RIAA)
Software Publishers Association (SPA)
Time-Warner, Inc.
U.S. Copyright Office
U.S. National Endowment for the Arts (NEA)
Viacom, Inc.

Prepared by the Educational Multimedia Fair Use Guidelines Development Committee, July 17, 1996
[Note: These guidelines were developed during the CONFU process but did not receive consensus support.]

APPENDIX H
Use of Copyrighted Computer Programs (Software) in Libraries—Scenarios

These scenarios illustrate some uses of computer programs and multimedia works by non-profit libraries, including those at nonprofit educational institutions, for administrative purposes and for on-site and off-site circulation, in light of the following provisions of the Copyright Act of 1976:

Section 107: Fair use privilege for certain unauthorized reproduction, distribution, adaptation, and public performance and display.

Section 109(b): Exemption from the software rental right for lending by nonprofit educational institutions, and exemption from the software rental right for lending by nonprofit libraries for nonprofit purposes.

Section 117: Exemption for archival "back-up" copies and adaptations essential for using computer program with machine.

Please note that the Guidelines for Classroom Copying in Not-for-Profit Educational Institutions are explicitly limited to books and periodicals, and do not encompass other types of copyrighted works, including computer programs.

1. **Library Administration**
   General Rule: Unauthorized reproduction, distribution, or adaptation of computer programs for library administration is governed by the same rules as other end-uses, and will be considered infringement unless it constitutes fair use under Section 107 or it is exempted under Section 117.
   a. A nonprofit university library purchases a spread sheet program for managing accounts payable, and the MIS director adapts the program so it can be used on the library's computers.

   This use qualifies for the Section 117 exemption. The owner of a lawfully acquired copy of a computer program is permitted to make an adaptation of a computer program "as an essential step in the utilization of the computer program in conjunction with a machine and that it is used in no other manner." If the library licenses, rather than purchases, the program, then it should refer to the license agreement or contact the copyright owner before making an adaptation.
   b. The administrator of a nonprofit university library licenses a spread sheet program for managing accounts payable, but the university business office uses a different program. The library administrator prepares monthly reports with the program,

which are sent to the university's business office on diskette or via e-mail with a copy of the library's spread sheet program.

No fair use defense or statutory exemption is available. Because the copy sent to the university business office was not lawfully made, this does not qualify for the nonprofit library lending exemption, or the nonprofit educational lending exemption permitting transfer of possession of computer programs to "faculty, staff, and students."

c. Assume the same facts as in (b) above, except that the library administrator does not send the monthly report with a copy of the library's spread sheet program, but rather reformats the monthly report in text for transmission to the university business office.

Fair use defense or statutory exemptions are not necessary. Because the library administrator has not made an unauthorized reproduction or distribution of the spread sheet program, it has not infringed the copyright.

d. A nonprofit library purchases a single-machine license for a spread sheet program to be used in calculating employee payroll. A library employee opens the sealed envelope containing the CD-ROM or diskette and installs the computer program on a computer without reading the license agreement. Later, he makes a copy of the program and gives it to a colleague on the library staff, who loads it on her computer.

No fair use defense exists under Section 107. The library has infringed the copyright by making an unauthorized reproduction of the computer program, and there are no other statutory exemptions available.

e. A librarian busy archiving the papers of a noted alumna decides to work at home. To keep track of his hours, he makes a copy of the spread sheet program installed on his office computer and takes it home to install on his home computer.

No fair use defense or statutory exemption is available. Because many end-users now want to work at home as well as the office, many business application publishers now offer "single user licenses," which permit the licensee to install and use the computer program on both an office and a home computer provided the two copies are not in use simultaneously.

f. A librarian licenses and installs a spread sheet program to manage her budget. Two years later, the librarian licenses a functional upgrade for the program, installs it on her office computer, and installs the older version alone on her home computer.

No statutory exemption or fair use defense exists if a valid license for the functional upgrade prohibits transfer of the older version to another machine or another user. Software license agreements distinguish between functional upgrades of licensed software and the current version licensed by new customers. Because functional upgrades are licensed on the assumption that the customer has already licensed a previous version of the software, their prices are usually about two-thirds lower than the price of the current title for new customers. Therefore, most functional upgrade licenses restrict or prohibit the transfer of the previous version to another user or machine.

There is disagreement about whether the same result would be reached if the functional upgrade and the older version are part of the library collection.

g. Assume the same facts as in (f), except that the librarian obtains a full price license to the new version of the program, rather than the less expensive functional upgrade, for her office computer, and installs the older version alone on her home computer.

It is unnecessary to consider fair use or statutory exemptions. Because the librarian has licensed two complete and independent programs, the copyright in the programs has not been infringed.

2. Lending Copies of Computer Programs to Library Patrons

General Rule: Provided that the required warning is placed on lawfully acquired copies of computer programs, they may be lent by nonprofit libraries to patrons for nonprofit purposes under Section 109(b) of the Copyright Act. In looking at these scenarios, keep in mind that the library patron may be liable for copyright infringement even if the library is not.

a. A nonprofit library possesses one copy of a popular word processing program pursuant to a valid license, affixes to the package the required copyright warning, and makes it available at the circulation desk for patrons to borrow.

This is permissible under Section 109(b)(2), provided that the lending library is unaware or has no substantial reason to believe that the computer software is lent for a for-profit purpose.

b. Assuming the same facts as in (a). A student working on an English literature research paper borrows the word processing program and installs it on her personal computer. Later, when the word processing program is overdue, she returns the packaged copy to the library, but keeps the copy installed on her computer to complete the research paper.

Statutory exemptions are available to the library, but not to the student. The Section 109(b)(2) lending exemptions permit "transfer of possession" and "lending" of computer programs by schools and libraries for users, but not unauthorized reproduction by patrons. The library would not face liability unless contributory infringement or vicarious liability is proved, such as demonstrating that the library encouraged patrons to copy.

c. A nonprofit library loans its copy of applications software that was purchased, not licensed. The required warning is affixed to the package.

This is permissible under 109(b)(2) provided that the borrowing library is unaware or has no substantial reason to believe that the software is to be used for for-profit purposes. Lending the applications software is impermissible if the library acquired it under a license which did not permit loans.

d. A library purchases a book with supplemental software on a disk in the book pocket. The library lends the book with the accompanying software in response to an interlibrary loan request.

This is permissible under Section 109(b)(2), provided that the book and software is lent for a nonprofit purpose, and the library affixes to the book or disk the required copyright warning.

3. Patron Use from Remote Servers

a. A library at a nonprofit educational institution obtains a single-machine license for a popular word processing program, but makes it available via a campus wide computer system that any number of students, faculty, and staff may access simultaneously from either on or off campus. The required copyright warning is displayed whenever an end-user signs onto the computer system.

The fair use defense and statutory exemptions are unavailable. The lending exemptions for nonprofit libraries and nonprofit educational institutions apply to lawfully made copies, but not to the unauthorized reproduction and public display that occurs with network distribution. The fair use defense also should not apply to this reproduction, despite its non-commercial purpose, because the entire computer program is reproduced, the computer program may be unpublished, and the serious commercial effect caused by lost license fees and pirated copies.

b. Assume the same facts as in (a), except that the library obtains a network version of the word processing program and a site license permitting simultaneous access for faculty, staff, and students.

There is no infringement by library or faculty, staff, or students.

c. A nonprofit library has installed a computer program on its network and made it available to patrons, pursuant to a license agreement, via on-site terminals. Despite warnings to the contrary, a patron copies the computer program onto a diskette for his personal use.

There is copyright infringement by the library patron, and neither the fair use defense nor a statutory exemption is available.

d. A student at a nonprofit educational institution licenses a computer program for her personal computer, and uploads the computer program to the school library's network, where it can be accessed and copied by several hundred students, faculty, and staff, without the permission of the copyright owner.

There is copyright infringement by the student. Her unauthorized reproduction of the computer program is not covered by Section 109(b) exemptions for nonprofit library lending for nonprofit purposes or nonprofit educational institutional lending.

Prepared by the Educational Multimedia Fair Use Guidelines Development Committee, July 17, 1996, Conference on Educational and Library Fair Use (CONFU).

GLOSSARY

accredited. Approved by a regional or national accrediting agency. Nonprofit educational institutions that qualify for the Technology, Education, and Copyright Harmonization (TEACH) Act exception must be accredited. K–12 schools are recognized as accredited by applicable state certification or licensing boards. Accredited higher educational institutions are approved by a regional or national accrediting agency recognized by the Council for Higher Education Accreditation or the U.S. Department of Education.

ASCAP (American Society of Composers, Authors, and Publishers). One of three performing rights societies that license rights to perform nondramatic musical works in the United States. *See also* **BMI**

BMI (Broadcast Music, Inc.). One of three performing rights societies that license rights to perform nondramatic musical works in the United States. *See also* **ASCAP; SESAC**

Chafee amendment. Section 121 of the copyright law, which allows for the making of accessible formats for people with disabilities under certain conditions.

circumvention. The act of bypassing a technological device or system (passwords, encryption, watermarking) to gain access to a work protected by copyright.

click-through license. A nonnegotiated license used with software and other electronic media. Acceptance of the license occurs when a customer clicks on or otherwise assents to the terms. Also called *click-wrap license. See also* **shrink-wrap license**

collected works. A compilation of several individual works that may each be protected by copyright.

common law. Law derived from judicial decisions.

compilation. A work made up of preexisting data or materials selected and arranged in a novel way that meets the creativity requirement for a work to be protected.

compulsory license. A license created by Congress that allows certain parties the right to use copyrighted works without prior permission of the copyright holder in exchange for a specific royalty fee.

Conference on Fair Use (CONFU). Meetings of copyright holders and user groups to discuss fair use issues and, where appropriate, fair use guidelines, convened by the Information Infrastructure Task Force, Working Group on Intellectual Property Rights, from 1994 to 1998.

contracts of adhesion. Contracts that allow for little or no opportunity to negotiate terms. *See also* **click-through license; shrink-wrap license**

contributory infringement. The act of contributing to or aiding the infringing acts of another person.

CONTU. *See* **National Commission on New Technological Uses of Copyrighted Works**

copyright. A set of exclusive rights awarded to a copyright holder for an original and creative work of authorship fixed in a tangible medium of expression. Copyright is a limited statutory monopoly that gives rights holders the sole right to market a work for a limited period of time. Copyright also includes exceptions to exclusive rights that permit a user of a copyright-protected work the right to exercise an exclusive right without authorization or royalty payment under certain conditions.

Copyright Clearance Center (CCC). A copyright royalty clearinghouse that collects permission fees for the use of copyrighted works (primarily journal articles) on behalf of publishers and other copyright holders. CCC also offers blanket license agreements to profit and nonprofit institutions for the use of copyrighted works.

copyright management information (CMI). Identifying information conveyed in connection with a work, such as title, author, copyright holder, terms of use, ISBN, and any other identifying information that may be required by the Register of Copyrights.

Creative Commons. A nonprofit organization that promotes the creative reuse of intellectual works, whether owned or in the public domain, through the use of licenses that define which rights copyright holders choose to retain and which rights they agree to waive so that others may use their work without prior permission.

de minimis. So trifling as to be not worth the effort to enforce or litigate.

derivative work. A copyrightable work such as a translation or dramatization that is based on an existing work. The right to create derivative works is an exclusive right of the copyright holder.

Digital Millennium Copyright Act (DMCA) of 1998. An amendment to the copyright law that sought to address new copyright concerns in the digital environment.

digital rights management (DRM). Defined by the National Institute of Standards and Technology as "a system of information technology components and services, along with corresponding law, policies and business models, which strives to distribute and control intellectual property and its rights. Product authenticity, user charges, terms-of-use and expiration of rights are typical concerns of DRM."

dramatic literary or musical work. A stage play, opera, musical, or similar work with a dramatic presentation. Compare **nondramatic literary or musical work**

EULA (End User License Agreement). An agreement associated with the use of digital information or products. *See also* **click-through license**

exceptions and limitations. Situations defined in copyright law where the general rules do not apply. Nonprofit educational institutions, libraries, and archives have several copyright exceptions allowing them to use works without the authorization of the rights holder.

exclusive rights. The rights of the copyright holder to reproduce, distribute, publicly perform, and display a work and to create derivative works based on the original.

fair use. An exception defined in section 107 of the copyright law allowing a user to exercise an exclusive right under certain circumstances without the prior authorization of the copyright holder and without paying a royalty or permission fee.

first sale. Under section 109 of the copyright law, an exception to the exclusive right of distribution that entitles the holder of a lawfully acquired copy of a protected work the right to sell, lend, or otherwise dispose of the copy.

fixed in tangible medium. Preserved in a perceptible, physical form, as the words inscribed in a book or the music encoded on a compact disc; one of the requirements for copyright protection.

grand performing rights. Contract rights associated with dramatic literary and musical works.

Harry Fox Agency. A copyright clearinghouse and licensing agency for the music industry.

IDEA (Individuals with Disabilities Education Act). A federal law addressing the educational needs of children with disabilities.

infringement. The act of violating one or more of a copyright holder's exclusive rights.

innocent infringement. Violation of copyright without the knowledge of having done so.

liability. Responsibility for an illegal offense enforceable by civil remedy or criminal punishment.

market failure. A situation where a consumer demand cannot be met, sometimes leading to government intervention.

mechanical license. In a contract, the right to make a recording of a musical performance.

National Commission on New Technological Uses of Copyrighted Works (CONTU). A group created by Congress in 1979 to address the use of new technologies. CONTU recommended that original and creative computer programs and new, original works created through the use of computers be afforded copyright protection and created guidelines addressing interlibrary loan and photocopying.

nondramatic literary or musical work. A novel, poem, song, musical composition, or similar work without a dramatic presentation. Compare **dramatic literary or musical work**

online service provider (OSP). In the DMCA, any entity that offers transmission and routing or provides connections for digital online communications but does not create or modify the content of material sent or received.

phonorecord. A tangible object from which sounds are fixed and can be heard, communicated, or distributed either directly or through the use of a machine.

plagiarism. The use of another's work in a manner that suggests it is one's own.

public display. Display of a work before a group larger than a family or a small group of friends or at a place open to the public.

public domain. The realm of works not protected by copyright.

public performance. Performance of a work before a group larger than a family or small group of friends or in a place open to the public.

remedies. The means through which a court can enforce copyright, as through statutory damages, injunctions, declaratory relief, and so forth.

rulemaking. A process initiated by a government agency to create or amend a rule or regulation.

safe harbor. A statutory or regulatory provision that prevents one from liability.

SESAC (Society of European Stage Authors and Composers). One of three performing rights societies that license rights to perform nondramatic musical works in the United States. *See also* **ASCAP; BMI**

shrink-wrap license. A nonnegotiated license enclosed in the packaging of some software and other products. Acceptance of the license terms occurs when a customer opens the shrink-wrap packaging. *See also* **click-through license**

Sonny Bono Copyright Term Extension Act of 1998. An amendment to the copyright law that extended the term of copyright protection by twenty years.

Statute of Anne. The British copyright act of 1710 that gave authors copyright protection for their works.

statutory damages. Legal penalty that, for copyright infringement, can range from $750 to $30,000 per work infringed.

synchronization license. A license to perform music in sync with a video, movie, television program, and so on.

technological protection measures (TPMs). Digitally implemented strategies, such as password protection and watermarking, used to control access to or copying of protected works.

Technology, Education, and Copyright Harmonization (TEACH) Act of 2002. An amendment to the copyright law that updated sections 110 and 112 to allow for the public performance and display of copyrighted work in digital forms and transferred through digital networks for teaching purposes at accredited nonprofit educational institutions.

thick copyright. An expression that refers to the greater protection afforded to unpublished works and to works that have a higher level of creativity than other copyrighted works.

time shifting. Copying a television program or other broadcast work to view or use at a later time.

transformative use. A use of a protected work that recasts it or uses it in a different way than originally intended by the rights holder.

vicarious infringement. Secondary copyright infringement wherein a person knows about the infringement and may benefit from it.

work for hire. A copyrightable work created by an employee or a contractor hired for that purpose.

INDEX

ABOUT THE AUTHOR

Carrie Russell is the director of the Program on Public Access to Information for the Office for Information Technology Policy of the American Library Association. Russell is a frequent speaker at state, regional, and national library conferences and the author of the best seller *Complete Copyright: An Everyday Guide for Librarians*, now in its second edition. She also pens a popular monthly column, "Carrie on Copyright," in *School Library Journal*. Russell works and lives in Washington, D.C.